A Portrait of Leadership

Raymond Delmut Na'anlep

Published By:

Ssali Publishing House

www.ssalipublishing.com

Publishing African Narratives by African Authors

Editor: Rose Ssali

ssalirose@gmail.com

Cell +27 71 726 8717

ISBN 978-1-990901-27-0

Printed in South Africa

Dedication

I dedicate this book to my parents, the first leaders
I observed and emulated
To My siblings who brought out the leader in me
By challenging me
Believing in me
And championing me

I dedicate it to my beautiful wife, Martina,
Whose leadership as a woman
Compassionate, gentle, forward-thinking
And an entrepreneurial leader
Complement my own brand of leadership
Making us a great team
And because of her love & commitment
To our heavenly Father
I walk in integrity and positivity.

Acknowledgements

I wish to acknowledge all the leaders from whom I have learned; those who have inspired me, motivated, and or challenged me. I recognize those who have led with integrity and those who continue to do so.

I applaud the youth who have taken the baton and with vision, energy and commitment seized their place in leadership, unapologetically.

Special thanks go to John Shama Shaga, Assistant Director, Embassy of Nigeria in Buenos Aires, for the encouragement and financial support he gave me towards editing my first book. He greatly influenced my venture into writing.

It is with sincere gratitude that I say thank you to my editor and publisher, Rose Ssali, managing director of Ssali Publishing House, for her encouragement, care and attention during the entire journey that saw this book go from an idea to a concept and finally to a book.

Contents

Introduction

In the advent of Covid-19, citizens in every country around the world looked to their leaders for decisive action, for guidance and hope that the sun would rise the next day.

On one hand, some leaders stood up, spoke authoritatively; eased the fears that were overwhelming the populace and brought a modicum of sanity during a very terrifying time. They were not saying they had the answers, that there was no crisis. Rather they reminded the nation that it was an extremely difficult time; sacrifices would need to be made and then invited the populace to stand with him or her so that together, they would overcome the crisis.

On the other hand, some leaders were nonchalant, even going as far as saying there was nothing to worry about even as the news and their advisors were indicating otherwise.

We are living through a global health crisis with no modern-day precedent. What governments, corporations, hospitals, schools, and other organizations need now, more than ever, are real leaders. We need men and women who will help us overcome the limitations of our own individual laziness, selfishness, weakness, and fear and get us to do better, harder things than we can get ourselves to do on our own.

I know that some exhibit natural traits of leadership but for many who have demonstrated strong leadership qualities, especially the ability to help others triumph over adversity, is not written into their genetic code. They are, instead, made. They are forged in crisis. Leaders become 'real' when they practice a few key behaviours that motivate and inspire people through difficult times. As Covid-19 tears its way through country after country, town after town, neighbourhood after neighbourhood, I thought it would be important for us to explore how some of history's iconic leaders acted in the face of great uncertainty, real danger, and collective fear.

Sadly, today many leaders ascend to power based on their sweet-talking or purchase of votes rather than on their proven track record to lead.

I write this book, firstly, to raise awareness as to the quality of leadership we need in order to attain the highest level of our humanity. Secondly, I write to urge you to be conscious and deliberate in your choice of leadership because therein lies the architects, to some degree, of your failure or success in fulfilling your destiny. Thirdly, I put pen to paper, to nudge you, in fact, to implore you to take up leadership at whatever strata of society you are at and make your meaningful contribution to a better world.

Here are some values that leaders have relied on for their sustained leadership:

Courage
Acknowledge people's fears, then encourage resolve

Most of us know the famous lines of U.S. President Franklin Delano Roosevelt's 1933 inaugural address in the midst of the Great Depression:

"The only thing we have to fear is…fear itself."

He followed that by pointing to the nation's strengths in meeting the crisis:

"This is no unsolvable problem if we face it wisely and courageously. There are many ways in which it can be helped, but it can never be helped merely by talking about it. We must act and act quickly."

Faith

Less than a decade later, as the United Kingdom stared down the Nazi onslaught in the Second World War, Prime Minister Winston Churchill encouraged his people to keep the faith:

"We shall not fail or falter; we shall not weaken or tire. Neither the sudden shock of battle, nor the long-drawn trials of vigilance and exertion will wear us down. Give us the tools, and we will finish the job."

In the business world, consider examples like Katharine Graham, leader of The Washington Post in 1971, who moved through her own fears by vowing that the free press would not cave to government demands to stop publication of the Pentagon Papers. She then helped her editors and journalists do the same, as the newspaper began printing a series of revelatory articles and excerpts about U.S. involvement in Vietnam.

Or think about Ed Stack, CEO of Dick's Sporting Goods, who, when confronted with the extraordinary increase in school shootings in the United States, persuaded his board and management team to risk the ire of gun rights' advocates and a significant decline in revenue by discontinuing the sale of firearms at its namesake stores.

Your job, as a leader today, is to provide both brutal honesty — a clear accounting of the challenges your locality, company, non-profit, or country faces — and credible hope that collectively you and your people have the resources needed to meet the threats you face each day: determination, solidarity, strength, shared purpose, humanity, kindness, and resilience.

Recognize that most of your employees are anxious about their health, their finances, and, in many cases, their jobs. Explain that you understand how scary things feel, but that you can work together to weather this storm.

If you're looking for in-the-moment role models, turn to Governor Andrew Cuomo of New York or Governor Gretchen Whitmer of Michigan, both of whom are offering de facto masterclasses in crisis leadership: explaining the gravity of the situations their states are facing, outlining the resources being deployed to battle the coronavirus, and calling their constituents to act from their stronger, more compassionate selves.

Inspire your followers with the words of the Reverend William Sloane: *"Courage is a crucial virtue. Will we be scared to death, or scared to life?"*

Give people a role and purpose
Real leaders charge individuals to act in service of the broader community. They give people jobs to do.

During the U.S. Civil War, for example, President Abraham Lincoln exhorted and ordered men of Northern states to fight; as the civil rights movement gathered momentum in the late 1950s and early 1960s, the Reverend Martin Luther King, Jr, asked his followers to sit in, march, and otherwise protest racial discrimination. In his first inaugural, FDR told his countrymen to keep their money in the banks as an important way of averting a banking crisis; later, his wife, First Lady Eleanor Roosevelt, encouraged American women to work in the nation's factories, while their fathers, brothers, husbands, and sons went to battle in the Second World War.

On a smaller scale, we can look to Antarctic explorer Ernest Shackleton's leadership. When, in 1915, his expedition ship The Endurance became stuck in the ice and he realized that he and his crew would have to wait out the brutal winter on a floating iceberg, he insisted that each man maintain his ordinary duties: sailors swabbed decks; scientists collected specimens; others were assigned to hunt for meat. He knew that daily routines and tasks, including manual labour, would help establish order and thus ground his men in an uncertain time that was filled with danger.

In the current crisis, leaders must act in a similar fashion — giving their followers direction and reminding them why their work matters. In organizations providing essential services, such as government agencies, hospitals, pharmacies, grocery stores, food and healthcare equipment manufacturing plants, news outlets, scientific labs, non-profits serving the poor and many others — this raison d' etre will be immediately apparent. But it's still vitally important to emphasize the key role that each person involved in the operation plays. And, in other businesses, the new mission can be as simple as helping all stakeholders navigate this crisis as effectively as possible. At a Nebraska truck stop, which

Karen Gettert Shoemaker's family has run for years, she and others are focusing on keeping the truckers who provide essential goods moving across the country, offering them a welcoming pitstop on their journeys.

When in doubt about what you or your team can do during this pandemic, prioritize helping others — even in the smallest ways. When I was going through a particularly difficult period in my life, I heard a sermon by Peter Gomes, who then ministered at Harvard's Memorial Church that reminded me of the transformative power of giving. "When in the midst of [outer] turmoil and calamity you seek the inner strength that helps you not only to endure but to overcome, do not look for what you can get," he told his audience. "Look rather for what you have been given, and for what you can give." When we help others, even in the smallest ways, our fear ebbs and our focus sharpens.

Emphasize experimentation and learning
To successfully navigate crisis, strong leaders quickly get comfortable with widespread ambiguity and chaos, recognizing that they do not have a crisis playbook. Instead, they commit themselves and their followers to navigating point-to-point through the turbulence, adjusting, improvising, and re-directing as the situation changes and new information emerges. Courageous leaders also understand they will make mistakes along the way and they will have to pivot quickly as this happens, learning as they go.

During his long, dark winter on The Endurance, Shackleton constantly responded to changing circumstances. When his ship got stuck, he shifted his mission from exploration to survival. When the ship was no longer habitable, he instructed his men to build a camp on the ice.

When he finally got his team to an uninhabited island, where he knew there was no chance of outside rescue, he and a small group of his men, sailed one of the three lifeboats 800 miles to another island, where he knew he could find help. Four months and three thwarted rescue attempts later, Shackleton finally arrived back to the original island to the rest of his team. They were all alive, and he brought them home.

During the Cuban Missile Crisis in late 1962, President John F. Kennedy demonstrated the same agility; at each juncture of the standoff between the United States and the Soviet Union; he ordered his small team of advisers to work to expand his options rather than committing to and blindly following one course of action.

Emphasize to your followers that you expect everyone — individually and as a group — to learn their way forward, to experiment with new ways of operating, to expect the occasional failure and then quickly pivot to a new tack, to figure out the future together. In fact, this crisis — including the social distancing measures it has required and the widespread economic downturn following closely in its wake — presents a powerful opportunity for organizations and teams of all kinds to better understand their strengths and weaknesses, what really engages and motivates their people, and their own reason for being.

Tend to energy and emotion — yours and theirs
Crises take a toll on all of us. They are exhausting and can lead to burnout. For many, who lose loved ones, it's devastating. Thus, one critical function of leadership during intense turbulence is to keep your finger on the pulse of your people's energy and emotions and respond as needed.

When tending to energy and emotion, you must begin with yourself. As a high-ranking executive commented before the pandemic,

"If you as the leader flag, everything flags. Everything else, including your organization's mission, becomes vulnerable."

So, in these trying times, take good care of yourself, physically, emotionally, and spiritually. Know when you are capable of being focused and productive, and when you need a break. Eat well, get enough sleep, exercise regularly, spend time outdoors (six feet away from strangers), connect in person with your partner, kids, or animals and virtually with friends and extended family, plan for at least two device-free periods per day (of a minimum of 30 minutes each), and rely on other practices that help you get grounded.

Lead with conviction and courage

There is plenty of boldness in leadership. But, sadly, there's too little courage. The greatest courage is not the courage to tell people what to do. It is the courage to tell yourself what to do. It is not the courage to attempt great things. It is the courage to bring your best self to daily challenges and opportunities.

The most surprising aspect of leadership is the courage it takes. You are not leading if you don't feel the need to act courageously. Every meaningful act of leadership requires courage.

Chapter 1

Leadership is a Lifestyle

Leadership needs everyone on board to play their role!
Raymond Delmut Na'anlep

The Covid-19 pandemic that has gripped the world has also made us reflect on life, on our purpose and therefore, not surprisingly on leadership. It has provided me with revelations hitherto never understood before. I now see some things with such clarity it is difficult to believe I did not see them in that light before. I woke up one morning and instantly, the movie Lion King played out in my mind. I recalled the lessons from the animal kingdom represented in the movie. Let me share them with you because they are so profound and because I believe by understanding these principles and values, together, we will make the difference Africa needs to keep rising.

Leadership does not belong to one person

Mufasa is the capable and undisputed king of Pride Rock, who enjoys grooming his son, Simba for the responsibility that lies ahead of him. Mufasa believes in succession planning and the only way to keep and protect the kingdom is to prepare the future leaders for the challenges and complexities of leadership. Sarabi, his loving and loyal wife, is with him on this journey. Though she is fine in the shadows of Mufasa, she is respected. Her quiet strength is known both by her family and the inhabitants of Pride Rock. Both parents join efforts to raise Simba to be who he needs to be.

Simba is destined to rule Pride Rock after his dad's demise. It is his inheritance to rule but he must learn the ropes. The position is hereditary, but the responsibility has to be learnt.

When Mufasa holds up the little cub, all the animals in the kingdom come out and stand in position. They are different species, different sizes, signifying different roles. They each have a role in keeping the kingdom going.

We see this in the escapades of Simba as he plays in the grass, frolicking with his friends who seem to have greater wisdom than he has despite his being the future king. They poke and nudge him about various things and from their conversations we can already see that we are influenced by those we have around us. The lesson here is that we must choose our friends carefully because of their influence on us. Simba is the future king but even then, sometimes the wisdom required comes from his buddies. A leader can't know everything, no way. However, if he has a good circle of friends around him, his leadership is so much better for their input and even more so because they are vested in his leadership and his image, for all their sakes.

Likewise, in the African setting, our leadership journey started with the name they gave you when you were born. Your mother took on her role in developing your leadership skills and this is how she did it. When she bathed you, she sang songs of bravery; when she carried you snuggly on her back, she talked of the places you would go and the feats of greatness you would achieve. She lovingly fed you from her own hand because to her you were royalty. From resting your head on her breast, you already learned gentleness and kindness that nothing could take away from you. It is not for nothing that it is referred to as the milk of human kindness.

When the time came, boys were sent to the men to learn other lessons but until you were of age, you came back to your mother's hut where you observed and heard words spoken, always to teach, to validate and to uplift you, the future leaders or the crucial support of leaders.

As a boy, your sisters gave you the opportunity to learn how to treat young women while the way you treated those older than you were lessons that contributed to your personal development. From their laughter you learnt that life is filled with joy; from their wistful ways you learned that life is something to be embraced.

Our western-style education eroded African training of its people. We were told that in the civilized world, education begins when you are five or seven years old. You go to class for a prescribed number of hours a day, and when you are younger that might only be from 9 am to 12 noon, just three hours.

In addition to this erroneous advice, parents were sold on the thinking that children cannot develop their intellect without expensive toys and other external items. The children have time allocated to creativity with items such as factory-made clay. In contrast, when Mama Njeri goes to the river to wash clothes, she puts her little one among the sun-kissed rocks. He and his little friends dig their chubby little hands into the mud and create little piles of mud from which they start creating things as they envision them, complete with earthworms wriggling to their delight. As they get older they create exotic things like cars and houses from whatever it is they find in their environment. The mothers, keeping a watchful eye smile and know that they have architects, contractors and farmers in the making. The children create their toys, balls and dolls from the items around them. When they are brought toys from the shop, they want to tear them apart and see how they function, but they are called destructive. Later in the Physics class, the teacher tells them about breaking down everything to its smallest element in order to then understand it best. The little child could have taught them that at the age of two because to him that came naturally.

Now let me let you in on a secret: an African child's training was round the clock. As they played they were in training and as the sun went down, the lessons peaked with the stories that they would take with them to sleep, internalize them so that they formed their dreams and became part of their psyche. Did you ever wonder why stories were told in the evenings? Well, that is the reason why! There were stories about everything, and the proverbs augmented the training of the African child.

Our western civilised education has a curriculum that indicates that learning has a beginning point and an end. In the African setting, my dear reader, learning is life-long. Sorry, you never graduate from the school of life; you enjoyed the learning and then you in turn, consistently taught, those around you. There are lessons for every eventuality and every season because there is a purpose for every season under heaven. (Ecclesiastes)

And when you got older, you joined Uncle Achukwu at his shop for an apprenticeship. He did not pay you but provided for your board and after a few years, he set you up to carry on business in the trade he had trained you in, so you did not worry about investor capital. Given this culture, unemployment was as foreign a concept as those who brought it to our shores.

There was no need for Labour Laws because training and developing the next generation was a duty and a privilege undertaken with pride. The quality of your leadership was measurable by the quality of those you had taken under your wing. They were your trophies and you were as proud of them as they were of you. You did your very best with those entrusted to you because as you trained their sons or daughters, someone was training yours in their field of interest and together as a village, we raised the next generation of leaders.

Chapter 2

Leadership Is Not Positional

"Leadership is not about a title or a designation. It's about impact, influence and inspiration."
Robin Sharma

Sarabi, the lioness, and Simba's mother was an understated leader in the movie. She was rarely seen but her impact and resilience in upholding the value of Mufasa's legacy was the platform that Simba rode on. Imagine if she had sold out. It would have been difficult for Simba to return. She knew her position in the kingdom and did not give up even when there was no hope in the horizon. Every one leads from a different place and strata. Leadership needs everyone on board to play their role.

This is a critical lesson on leadership: leadership is not about positions. Just because someone occupies a position of leadership does not mean they are leading. In reality, many people have been in a "position" of leadership but have never led a day in their life.

What do I mean? Leaders don't just occupy positions they exert influence in order to effect change. They influence people to achieve a common goal. They influence people to deliver excellence. They influence communities and organizations in a way that makes a positive impact. Ultimately, leaders influence by the way that they carry themselves and treat people. They lead by example.

John Maxwell says,
"Leadership is influence. Nothing more, nothing less."

That's a simple way of looking at leadership, but when you strip it down, that's what leadership is all about — influencing.

What this also means is that you do not have to be in a formal position of leadership to actually lead, you can and should influence others where you are now. Do not let your lack of positional authority inhibit your ability to make a difference. You can lead where you are, and you can have a significant impact on the people around you and the organization of which you are a part — that's leadership.

So instead of focusing on the position you do or do not have, how about focusing on your ability to influence others in a positive and significant way? This is a personal challenge I have set for myself so as I write this book, it is an exploration of leadership for myself as much as it is a shared journey that I hope I will play my leadership role in influencing you and others along the way so that together we make the real difference.

I started off by asking myself this critical question:
Na'anlep, why do you want to lead? What difference do you want to make?

Leadership has become trendy and many want to be leaders but don't necessarily have compelling reasons. Leadership should be borne out of a desire to contribute rather than simply achieve. Leadership done right benefits both the leader and the greater good: followers, the organization, and or the community. Know why you want to lead because without compelling reasons, you probably won't be able to pay the cost of developing your leadership abilities and maintain your commitment in the face of challenges.

For instance, in my own office and among my colleagues, I try to do my very best because I know that doing so enables the whole Mission to run smoothly. When the Mission runs seamlessly, it has a direct bearing on our country's nationals that are living here in South Africa and secondly, it has a bearing on the relations between our host nation and our home country.

On the other hand, at home, I join hands with my wife to be co-leaders for the good of our family, knowing that the foundation we provide will have far-reaching effects on our own.

Next, I learned to look for opportunities to lead. Don't wait for someone to bring them to you. What needs to be done at your organization? What problems need solutions? What opportunities could be seized? What could be improved? Initiative is a pre-requisite to effective influence. Look around. Pay attention. Get involved.

Finally, be willing to do what others aren't. Work a little harder and smarter, prepare a little more, and study a little more deeply. If you're asked to do something, consider it an opportunity to improve your leadership abilities and deliver results that will showcase your abilities and prove you are a leader. In most organizations, these opportunities are presented to us every day but because they do not come with titles, we often miss them. Keep your eyes open, you will begin to notice every day and more so, your bosses, on seeing your willingness will give you more opportunities that will develop your leadership skills even more.

The circumstances we are living in have caused many people to feel disconnected from the workplace. However, there are things leaders can do to encourage their people to take more personal responsibility for the organization's success.

First, as a leader, be clear on what those you lead are responsible for. Followers need a clear focus on what they are accountable for doing and the kind of results they are expected to consistently achieve.

Second, consider the fit between the person and the task. One nuance of good leadership is matching not just the right people to the right job, but the best person to a particular job. "Best" is usually the person with the skills and interest, not just the ability to do the work.

Third, don't overlook a discussion of consequences. People are accountable to the degree they feel they are going to experience a benefit or avoid a negative. If not taking responsibility has the same outcome as taking responsibility, why bother?

In our current circumstances, I have realized the importance of giving people hope, which I define as having something new to try and being willing to try it. There is no hopeless situation if you can find something different to try and you are willing to act on the idea.

Leaders inspire us to keep searching for new solutions and don't let lack of past success in dealing with a problem trick you into thinking there's nothing you can do. Indeed, great leaders help people have a larger vision of themselves. Leaders look for the potential in followers that followers often don't recognize in themselves.

I am a testament of the truth that if you expect more from those you lead you will get more. Don't be delusional and expect the impossible or you run the risk of demoralizing those you lead. Knowing your boss or project leader believes in you makes you strive harder to get the job done; I know this for a fact about myself.

I learned a great technique from sports: Connect behaviour with outcomes. Show your followers evidence of how their work impacts others, like customers and colleagues. Create a connection between what they do and the kind of difference they make. For instance, if your goalie does not protect the goal then regardless of how good your striker is, you will have so many goals scored against you, your striker has no chance to show how good he is on the other side of the field.

There is a young female basketball player whose story I found fascinating. In the championship game, her team was down by twelve points with less than six minutes to go. As point guard she called for time out. When the game resumed, it was an electrifying six minutes. Her team won the Championship by SIX POINTS.

Asked what she had said to the team during that time out, her answer was,
"I said to them that I was going to win this championship game, but I needed each one of them to come along with me."

To the shouts of "Offence! Offence!" her players were relentless; they boxed in and they boxed out. They gave up nothing and they took everything from their opponents. It seemed her words, "I AM GOING TO TAKE THIS GAME…I NEED YOU!" moved their feet across the gym at lightning speed. No sooner did an opponent have the ball, this magical point guard unapologetically 'stole' it, twirled and passed it to her own shooting guard; with precision they moved in one fluid movement, all five of them, not just two or three but the entire squad of five moved as one. They covered the deficit and gained an additional six points just by two three-pointers. Our Point Guard took the game, but she did not do it alone. She got her whole team to play ball, to take ownership of the championship game and together, THEY WON!

In the current pandemic, our political leaders need to rally their followers, the citizenry more than ever. The success of any policy depends almost entirely on the people heeding the guidelines and taking ownership of the game. If this happens, it doesn't matter how the number of cases are stacked against us; we will prevail and do so by a huge margin because we must, because we want the win even more desperately than the political leadership, because everything we are about depends on this win.

We must not forget this one truth:
"Leadership is not a person or a position. It is a complex moral relationship between people based on trust, obligation, commitment, emotion, and a shared vision of the good." ~ Joanne B. Ciulla, author and professor in ethics and leadership

Chapter 3

Integrity is the Hallmark of Leadership

"Integrity without knowledge is weak and useless, and knowledge without integrity is dangerous and dreadful."
Samuel Johnson

Integrity in leaders refers to being honest, trustworthy, and reliable. Leaders with integrity act in accordance with their words and own up to their mistakes, as opposed to hiding them, blaming their team, or making excuses.

If there is one thing the world needs in its leaders today, more than ever, it is integrity. It is one quality that sets leaders apart and they either have it or they don't.

Very simply put, integrity is synonymous with honesty and having strong moral values. In fact, the Random House Dictionary defines integrity as:

Adherence to moral and ethical principles; soundness of moral character; honesty.

Integrity is a valuable characteristic that true leaders must possess. This means following moral and ethical convictions, and doing the right thing always, even if it is unpopular, or even when no one is watching you. Leaders who have integrity never have to wonder about skeletons in their closets for there are none.

In the movie Lion King, we meet Scar, Mufasa's brother. We don't trust him from the outset. His lack of integrity leads him to kill his own brother because of his own insatiable desire to be king. He wants total power, just to have it. He shows no concern for the Pride Lands. Individuals with personalized power are selfish, impulsive, lack self-control, and are uninhibited. Scar deceived his family and the Pride Lands by placing the blame on Simba. Individuals with a personalized power motive are concerned with dominating others and having submissive followers. When the Pride Lands were in dire need of food, Scar refused to make the changes that were required to save the pack of lions. He would rather let them starve just to maintain his control over them.

As leaders, there will be many occasions when your integrity will be tested. People you care about will, knowingly or unknowingly, present situations that could compromise your integrity. You have to be vigilant and look at each situation carefully and never leave things to chance.

A good friend and I were surmising about leadership in Africa and the discussion turned to how our parents, being old-school, could not fathom being part of the corrupt activities that we see so often playing out in scandals in various countries today.

She shared with me the fact that her father had been in charge of awarding scholarships to civil servants to pursue post-graduate degrees. Two years after she joined the Department of Foreign Affairs, she told her father that she wanted to apply for her master's degree. He responded that she did not qualify because she needed to work for the department for at least three years. Secondly, he pointed out that she would need to apply through her department head and have them recommend her for further studies. Third, he reminded her that the reason there was need for her to work the prescribed number of years was because there were others ahead of her. He recounted that it takes all decks on hand to run a department or organization and if each one only thought of themselves and not the whole team, then that boat would be doomed from the start. It was a lesson well taught.

Eventually, she did earn her scholarship, was recommended by her head of department and in fact, her scholarship did not come through the government. Her father encouraged her to submit applications directly to foreign universities. She took study leave and upon graduation got several job offers from international organizations. Her father would hear none of it and prevailed upon her to come back and work for two years to honour the fact the department had paid her while she was on study leave. Would anyone have pursued her for that detail in her employment contract? Probably not, but again, as her father taught her, did she want to live the rest of her life wondering whether her error would catch up with her? Why not just do the right thing and never have to wonder about it!

That man had integrity and his character was unquestionable. As he said to his daughter,
"Not only must you do what is right, you must be seen to do what is right."

This was a man who not only chose to live right, he taught his child the importance of integrity even where that lesson meant she did not get what she wanted when she wanted it. Today she is doubly thankful for the lesson.

Integrity also involves following company policies, appropriately using company time and resources, and respecting one's colleagues. It is important to remember that a leader's behaviour reflects not only on their own reputation but also on the reputation of the organization.

Integrity provides several benefits to both leaders and the organizations. For instance, research has linked greater integrity with increased workplace performance. Additionally, leaders with integrity foster greater trust and satisfaction from their direct reports, who are more likely to follow suit. Employees serving under high integrity leaders demonstrate more positive workplace behaviour and fewer negative workplace behaviour such as falsely calling in sick. Moreover, employees who trust their leaders to have integrity are likely to work harder, perform better, and have greater company loyalty.

In assessing your level of integrity, ask yourself the following questions:

- Am I accountable for my behaviour and the decisions I make?
- Do I accept responsibility for my mistakes?
- Am I setting a good example for my direct reports?
- Do I always follow through on my commitments and promises?
- Do I act in ways that build trust with those I lead?

So now that we know what integrity is and we know it is desirable, how do we develop our leadership skills?

Cultivate a good reputation:

A leader's reputation is based on more than performance. A good reputation also stems from being perceived as honest, responsible, reliable, and respectful by one's co-workers and direct reports. Remember that while it takes time and effort to build a good reputation, that reputation is easily damaged by negative behaviour. Because a leader's behaviour also influences the company's reputation, it is especially important to always act responsibly, respectfully, and ethically.

Consistency is key:

It is difficult to have faith in a leader who says one thing but does another: a leader's words and actions should match. Similarly, leader behaviour should be in line with company values and policies; otherwise it sends the message to direct reports that these are not important. On the other hand, leaders who consistently act with integrity can inspire direct reports to follow their example.

Hold yourself to a high moral standard:

Leaders with integrity do what is morally and ethically right and avoid questionable practices. For example, when making decisions, they consider potential consequences on the organization and other people. Acting with integrity also includes working diligently rather than cutting corners, accepting responsibility for decisions, and being honest and open with co-workers and direct reports.

Set a good example:

As a leader, it is your responsibility to be a good role model for your direct reports. Engaging in negative workplace behaviour such as disregarding company policies, gossiping about colleagues, using company time for personal matters, signals to direct reports that this behaviour is acceptable whereas it really is not acceptable by any standards. This may lead to other consequences. Employees who lack integrity are more likely to engage in unethical or counterproductive behaviours, which hurts both the work environment and the company.

However, leaders who act responsibly, make ethical decisions and uphold company values, help set and maintain expectations for employee conduct.

Here are two tales often told to teach about integrity:

The first version: There once was a boy who lived with his mother and father. Their family was poor. The father got a job with a company that processed mangos. The man thought the rich owner of the business would not miss a few mangos. So, the father stole three mangos one day for himself, his wife, and their boy. He said to his wife and boy: "What difference do three mangos make to the business? The owner will not miss them and we like mangos." The boy knew that his father did not pay for the mangos, but he ate one anyway because he was hungry. The father continued to bring three stolen mangos home to his family every day and they continued to eat the stolen mangos. The boy grew up and had a wife and a boy of his own. He got a job with a company that builds bridges and helped to build a long bridge across a large river. He thought that the rich owner of the bridge-building business would not miss a few building materials.

So, while he was working on the bridge, he stole materials to build a house for his family. Because he took many materials that were supposed to be part of the bridge, it lacked structural integrity when it was finished. Many people (including the man's wife and boy) celebrated the completion of the bridge by gathering together on the bridge for a ceremony. However, because the bridge lacked materials that were supposed to be used on it, it was not as strong as it looked. It collapsed during the ceremony and everyone—including the man and his family—were very sad.

The second version of this story: There once was a boy who lived with his mother and father. Their family was poor. The father got a job with a company that processed mangos. The man thought the rich owner of the business would not miss a few mangos. So, the father stole three mangos one day for himself, his wife, and their boy. He said to his wife and boy: "What difference do three mangos make to the business? The owner will not miss them and we like mangos." The boy and his mother knew that his father did not pay for the mangos, so they told him that they would not eat the mangos and that he should return them. The boy's father at first was angry, but after he thought about it he realized that his wife and son were right, so he agreed.

The next day he returned the mangos to the business owner and felt good inside. Over time, the owner noticed the man was honest and because he could trust him, he promoted him to have a better paying job at the mango processing plant. The boy grew up and had a wife and a boy of his own. He got a job with a company that builds bridges and helped to build a large bridge across a large river. He wanted to take some of the bridge building materials to build a house for his family but remembered the lesson his father had taught him by returning the mangos many years before, so the boy (now a man) resisted the temptation to take any of the building materials for his own house. When it was finished, it was built with all the necessary materials and had structural integrity. Many people (including the man's wife and son) celebrated the completion of the bridge by gathering together on the bridge for a ceremony. It was a beautiful day and the man felt very happy and proud.

Take responsibility for your actions:

Emily worked for one of the top travel agencies. She had demonstrated great skill in handling clients' requests and any problems that arose which is very common in the travel industry. Her bosses recognized her, and she quickly rose up the ranks to senior manager. When she had her twins, the company suggested she work from home to support their three branches. This was ideal for Emily's young family and she resolved to make the company proud of her. She knew her work ethic was unquestionable.

Unfortunately, there are many things we must keep an eye on as leaders. The company gave Emily a brand-new laptop and enough data every month so her support of the three branches would be seamless. On a few evenings when her husband did not have data, he asked if he could 'use' her laptop. She did not pay too much attention and it became quite common for them to share her work laptop.

One day Emily got a call from her boss who asked her to come into the office for a meeting. She was excited and believed that she was most likely getting a promotion. Imagine her shock and disbelief when they told her that disciplinary action was being taken against her for using company-provided data to watch porn movies on the company laptop. The company had a policy that mandated their data-provider to flag any employee that was using company time and or resources for nefarious activities.

Could Emily try to explain that it was not her but her husband? She was ultimately responsible for her workstation and the company's resources and as a true leader she took the reprimand. Over the next two years she was vigilant and never once, did anyone use her work laptop no matter the excuse.

Everyone makes mistakes, and not everything always goes according to plan. Rather than conceal mistakes or pin the blame on others, take responsibility. Fix mistakes if possible and if not, learn how to prevent them in the future. Finally, accepting responsibility for your own errors shows you care. This generates trust with your direct reports, and also encourages direct reports to be more open about their own mistakes.

Honour your commitments:
It is challenging to earn trust and respect from direct reports if you are unreliable. They want to know that if you make a promise, you'll keep it. This includes meeting deadlines, holding yourself to your word, and fulfilling commitments to coworkers and direct reports. Similarly, recognize your limitations and don't over-commit. It is far better to say no than it is to fail to follow through on a promise.

All said and done, personal integrity is an inborn moral conviction to do what is right, and reject that which is wrong, regardless of the consequences that are attached to their decisions.
According to Dan Coughlin, keynote speaker, management consultant and executive coach, there are three types of integrity:

Internal integrity - This is your integrity at the deepest level. Is your integrity just for show because it looks good, or do you truly live your life with integrity in mind? Internal integrity is about being able to do the right thing, even if no one is looking and even if you will receive absolutely no credit for doing so. Doing the right thing, even though it may be the harder option, despite no one looking will really be a huge step towards ensuring that you live with integrity.

External integrity - This is what you portray to those around you. You have high external integrity when your actions are consistent with your thoughts and what you are saying. If you are saying one thing, but your actions say something else - you have some more work to do!

Image integrity - Similar to external integrity - this is the image of your integrity. Whilst you might outwardly be displaying the right actions and taking the right path, can these actions be thought of in any other way? Are you leaving your image open to interpretation? People have great imaginations. When we don't understand something, we are very quick to make assumptions and form beliefs about why something is occurring. Looking after your image integrity is about ensuring that none of your actions or words can be misconstrued.

Why is Integrity Important?

Primarily, integrity is very important as these traits foster a positive workplace culture, one where there is open communication, good decision making and a strong moral compass guiding all decisions and actions. Whereas irresponsible behaviour and distrust can make a work environment uncomfortable and tense.

If you are known for your integrity, you will gain trust and respect from the people around you. Integrity is not just important on a personal level it is also vitally important at a workplace level. Organisations known for their integrity perform better.

I found that as leaders, we have many opportunities to demonstrate our integrity. However, by the same token, there are just as many opportunities to neglect our sense of honesty if we are that way inclined.

Here are some ways in which you can demonstrate your integrity as a leader:

Build Trusting and Respectful Relationships - Trust and respect are the ingredients of a healthy, positive workplace culture. Polite communication, respecting your colleagues' thoughts and ideas and continuously working on relationships demonstrates that you are a team player. Working as a team builds up trust and also shows that people can rely on you.

Communicate Openly and Honestly - Open and honest communication is the way to ensure that people know exactly what is going on around them, where everybody stands and the best way forward.

Follow Company Policies and Follow the Law - Policies are designed to guide you as to the best practice. If you choose not to follow them or if you use shortcuts, it will lead to bad decisions, problems and mistakes that will need fixing.

It is perhaps in sports that I saw this demonstrated very clearly. Soccer is a favourite pastime in my country and most African countries.

Coaches work hard to ensure their players are picked for the national squad. However, it is here that integrity is sometimes swapped in the name of winning.

I recall an incident whereby a coach had fielded a young player as Under 17 whereas he was actually Under 19. Previous records showed that he had already played in the Under 17 two years earlier. He was disqualified and banned from playing competitively for the next two years. There was also a fine of US$10,000.00 which, of course, was too much of a burden for his family. The young boy, distraught at the shame he had brought upon his family sought to take his own life.

In retrospect, the coach was saddened by what his lack of integrity had done. The ripple effect of his lack of integrity had far-reaching consequences.

Demonstrate Responsible Behaviour - Ensure that there is no reason for your colleagues to ever question your conduct by demonstrating ethical and moral behaviour at all times. This includes avoiding using the company's equipment or resources for personal use, striving to complete your task before deadlines and showing enthusiasm and commitment to your work.

Work Diligently - This is a very powerful way of demonstrating integrity as it shows that you are responsible for your work time. Focusing on your job responsibilities while at your desk will show your colleagues, manager, and even customers, that you have strong work ethics.

Sadly, today people take extreme liberties in their workplace. It is not uncommon to find people downloading movies and even watching movies online when they should be working. Social Media engagement is so distractive, taking away hours of productive time while people do not see the cost to their companies. Taking small things from the office such as a USB 'borrowed' that is never returned are a huge dent to our integrity if we do not look out.

Lead by Example - This sets a firm foundation for what you value most and how you want to work. By seeing you working by the same standards and expectations, it encourages others to follow suit.
Perhaps our mothers take the crown for doing this at home so that we get this lesson way before we leave home. They wake up earlier than anyone else, they make sure everybody's needs are taken care of and they do this with a smile and love.

Stand Up for Your Beliefs - This is about standing up for what you believe is the right way of doing things, even if everyone else is doing something different. As a leader, you never follow the crowd. The excuse that everybody is doing something does not cut it with leadership. A leader does what is right, not convenient or popular.

Have Your Own Identity - Come to understand who you are, what you are capable of becoming, what you want out of life and where you want to go. Ensure that these are not merely reflections of what others expect or want. Once you know this, align your values to this path and steer straight in all that you do.

At times, you may reach a point where you are asked to do something that doesn't go in accordance with your personal code of conduct. This may present a challenging decision for you, but if you have strong integrity and values, you will refuse to do it. Having the courage to say no is an important skill to learn.

"Have the courage to say no. Have the courage to face the truth. Do the right thing because it is right. These are the magic keys to living your life with integrity." ~ W. Clement Stone

A person of integrity shows a principled dedication to values and beliefs. They always reflect like a mirror.

In every relationship, even it is love, friendship, or a business relationship, the first question that someone asks is, "Can I trust you?" This trust is directly connected to integrity. Every worthy relationship is built on trust.

Having integrity means you live your life according to your deepest values, live with honesty and you keep your word every time. Your actions with integrity give you peace of mind in knowing you did the right thing regardless of the outcome. Choose your words and actions with your beliefs, values, and morals.

"The greatness of a man is not in how much wealth he acquires, but in his integrity and his ability to affect those around him positively." ~ Bob Marley

Your integrity is your most trusted friend as it keeps you on the right path. Make it your goal to be a person of integrity always no matter how many temptations or challenges you face.

Chapter 4

Sacrifice is at the Heart of leadership

"Leadership is about what you give up, not just what you take on…"
Unknown

What made Nelson Mandela's leadership was the unparalleled sacrifice people felt he had made for his country and for the cause he believed in. His stature was larger than life and it is undisputed that his sacrifice was more than many are called to make or would even be able to make if called on to do so.

For 20 years, he directed a campaign of peaceful, nonviolent defiance against the South African government and its racist policies. He gave up family, freedom; in actual fact, all the things we want for ourselves. He willingly gave up for himself what he knew was desirable so that others might have it. Decades-long incarceration on Robben Island with no hope of parole is more than many of us can fathom. That is leadership.

By the same token, Mother Teresa's leadership style took the world's attention on one singular word: Sacrifice! She could have raised funds around the world and sent missionaries to care for the poor and the sick. No, for a leader such as she was that would have been too easy. She chose to live among the poor, the sick and the dying. She did not eat gourmet meals and find cheap food for those she served. She ate what they ate; lived in the slums among the poorest of the poor and even when she got sick, she found solace in the clinics she had created for the poor of Calcutta. Her life demonstrated what sacrifice in leadership is all about in a way the world had never seen.

More recently, a young woman showed the world what leadership truly is. As a young girl, Malala Yousafzai defied the Taliban in Pakistan and demanded that girls be allowed to receive an education. She was shot in the head by a Taliban gunman in 2012 but survived. For years her father, a passionate education advocate himself, ran a learning institution in the city, and school was a big part of Malala's family. So, she already had the opportunity for education, this was not for herself. She was fighting for the rights of other young girls, even when her own life was at risk.

Given this backdrop of leaders who sacrificed so much, can we do any less in our own spheres of influence? We might never be called to make monumental sacrifices that put our lives in danger or where we give up everything but there is always something to be given up, always.

Regardless of the type of sacrifice, every leader must be willing to make sacrifices, because leaders are expected to pay the price others won't pay. That's what makes you the leader! But it's not just about making the hard decisions—good leaders make the hard decisions when they need to be made. Being able to face the moment of decision and choose the hard path of sacrifice in that moment defines the greatest leaders in history.

I cannot think of sacrifice and leadership and not think of the late Kobe Bryant. Everybody admired Kobe's game. We celebrated his ability, particularly his shot that many times carried his team through the Final Four to the Championship Game, bringing the victory home to the LA Lakers team many times over the years.

Tales of Bryant's work ethic have become folklore. From his early morning workouts, to marathon shooting sessions, to a relentless desire to improve himself, Kobe made the requisite sacrifice. In high school, he would show up at 5am for practice while everyone else showed up at 7am. Former NBA player and Lakers teammate John Celestand said Kobe was always the first player in the gym, even when he was hurt. Celestand once wrote that during the 1999-2000 season, Kobe broke his wrist. Celestand was excited because he thought with Kobe injured, he could beat him to the gym in the morning, particularly because Bryant lived over 30 minutes away from the practice facility. Instead, when he got in the next morning, Kobe was already in a full sweat with a cast on his right arm and dribbling and shooting with his left.

Great leaders also know what to give up. True leaders make sacrifices and forego things those they lead don't, shouldn't, or wouldn't want to give up.

As I have studied leaders over many years, I have seen leaders who have made tremendous sacrifices, and this has filled me with great respect and admiration for them. They have inspired me to seek ways in which I, too, can make sacrifices when my position demands it. Here are some ways I have personalized this aspect of leadership to enable my own leadership path:

Self-interest:

First and foremost, great leaders give up self-interest. I'm not saying they don't want to grow and advance or that they're martyrs. I'm saying they lift as they climb. They realize it's not about them and that they are guides to greatness and there to help others become the best version of themselves.

Credit:

Some of the bosses I have had the privilege of working with demonstrated a trait I found really admirable. If something went wrong and the Mission had to give account, they took the responsibility and blame for it. However, when we hosted major events and credit was being lavished, they directed the praise to their staff, pointing out various staff members who had outdone themselves. I realized that these were leaders who were secure in themselves and wanted the glow of success to shine on their team rather than on themselves. True leadership, in my book.

Their best people:

Great leaders willingly give up their best people to promotions and great career opportunities. In fact, they groom their employees for it and help facilitate it when the time comes. This is as opposed to leaders who keep talent down so they can selfishly keep them working to make them look good (which happens too often).

There is no successful leadership without sacrifice. If you think about life's great achievements; graduation, marriage, career; each comes with an equally enormous amount of sacrifice. Even the most successful people we can think of, such as Kobe whom I gave as an example, must put in long hours and give up the luxury of living a normal life to get where they are.

Leaders are often asked to give up more than others. When you have no responsibilities, you have total freedom to do whatever you want. However, the higher you climb on the leadership ladder, the more responsibilities you acquire and the more sacrifices you must make.

You must keep giving up to stay up. Short-term sacrifices are easy to justify but look at the many years Mother Teresa lived in the slums of Calcutta; the 27 years Nelson Mandela spent in prison. People are willing to put in long hours if it means they'll get a quick promotion. However, to continue moving up the ladder, you must continue to make sacrifices. Leadership success requires continual change, constant improvement, and ongoing sacrifice.

The higher the level of leadership, the higher the sacrifice. No matter your industry or career path, increasing leadership means increasing sacrifice. You must be prepared to give up your free time, your family time, and sometimes even your dream in order for the collective dream to manifest.

The first question you need to ask yourself as a leader is this: how much are you willing to sacrifice for your company? If you are not willing to work more than 40 hours a week, take a pay cut, or give up your vacation time, that's fine, but you need to accept that you are limited in how far you can advance on the leadership ladder.

If you are determined to advance, make a list of the things you are NOT willing to sacrifice. This could be your health, your marriage, or time with your kids. Then make a list of what you have to give up. Can you give more of your time, energy, or other resources to boost the organization's success? What do you have to offer?

Finally, keep in mind that to be a great leader, the sacrifice never ends. Many people assume that once they get that next promotion, their routine can go back to "normal." Being a great leader means continual sacrifice to become the best version of yourself. That's at the heart of the Law of Sacrifice.

Chapter 5

Servant Leadership is a Natural Trait

"Real leaders are not blinded by the trappings of power, but recognize their role as servant."
Archbishop Desmond Tutu

A Servant Leader shares power, puts the needs of the employees first and helps people develop and perform as highly as possible. Servant leadership inverts the norm, which puts the customer service associates as the main priority. Instead of the people working to serve the leader, the leader exists to serve the people. But, apart from being a thoughtful leadership approach, Servant Leadership can also function as a way of life, a life devoted to the service of others based on compassion, encouragement, selflessness and effective communication.

Back to our reference movie, Lion King, Sarabi kept the pride intact even in hard times. She did not leave them to the mercies of Scar when things got rough. She kept her loyalty to what was true. Her reluctance to join forces with Scar to ravish the kingdom was remarkable. It was a tough call, but she was loyal to the philosophies that she and her family believed, the circle of life. The circle of life signifies nature's way of taking and giving back and symbolizes life as being both divine and sacred. Scar built his own bridges and used them but as you know, evil can only reign for a time. Scar fulfilled his promise to the hyenas (mercenaries). He told them, *"When I am king, the mighty will be able to take whatever they want."* But when things went south, they had him for a meal.

Many mothers exhibit servant leadership to their families. A servant leader's focus is primarily on other people's well-being and growth. The servant leader isn't a sole leader with power, but rather, a power-sharer. They put other people's needs above their own and enable their team to grow, develop and perform to the best of their ability.

My mother, God rest her soul in eternal peace, was definitely a servant leader. I believe, like many mothers in our community, her desire to see her children grow and do well motivated her to work even when she was too tired to keep going; she would feed us and only eat once we had eaten our fill. She prayed over us, tried her best, always, to make sure that we were comfortable before thinking of her own comfort. She talked about the opportunities we would have to be our best and never once did she make reference to her own dreams or comfort.

The qualities that made my mom and the mothers in my community are listening, empathy, healing, awareness, persuasion, conceptualization, foresight, stewardship, commitment to the growth of people and building community.

Here are several characteristics that I view as being of critical importance, central to the development of servant leaders. My own work currently involves a deep understanding of the following characteristics and how they contribute to the meaningful practise of servant leadership. These characteristics include:

Listening

Leaders have traditionally been valued for their communication and decision-making skills. Although these are also important skills for the servant leader, they need to be reinforced by a deep commitment to listening intently to others. The servant leader seeks to identify the will of a group and helps to clarify that will. He or she listens receptively to what is being said and what is being left unsaid. Listening also encompasses hearing one's own inner voice. Listening, coupled with periods of reflection, is essential to the growth and well-being of the servant leader.

Empathy

The servant leader strives to understand and empathize with others. People need to be accepted and recognized for their special and unique spirits. One assumes the good intentions of co-workers and colleagues and does not reject them as people, even when one may be forced to refuse to accept certain behaviours or performance. The most successful servant leaders are those who have become skilled empathetic listeners.

Healing

The healing of relationships is a powerful force for transformation and integration. One of the great strengths of servant leadership is the potential for healing one's self and one's relationship to others. Many people have broken spirits and have suffered from a variety of emotional hurts. Although this is part of being human, servant leaders recognize that they have an opportunity to help make whole those with whom they come in contact.

Awareness

General awareness, and especially self-awareness, strengthens the servant leader.

Persuasion

Another characteristic of servant leaders is reliance on persuasion, rather than on one's positional authority, in making decisions within an organization. The servant leader seeks to convince others, rather than coerce compliance. This particular element offers one of the clearest distinctions between the traditional authoritarian model and that of servant leadership. The servant leader is effective at building consensus within groups.

Conceptualization

Servant leaders seek to nurture their abilities to dream great dreams. The ability to look at a problem or an organization from a conceptualizing perspective means that one must think beyond day-to-day realities. For many leaders, this is a characteristic that requires discipline and practice. The traditional leader is consumed by the need to achieve short-term operational goals.

The leader who wishes to also be a servant leader must stretch his or her thinking to encompass broader-based conceptual thinking. Within organizations, conceptualization is, by its very nature, a key role of boards of trustees or directors. Unfortunately, boards can sometimes become involved in the day-to-day operations—something that should be discouraged—and thus, fail to provide the visionary concept for an institution.

Trustees need to be mostly conceptual in their orientation, staff need to be mostly operational in their perspective, and the most effective executive leaders probably need to develop both perspectives within themselves. Servant leaders are called to seek a delicate balance between conceptual thinking and a day-to-day operational approach.

Foresight

Closely related to conceptualization, the ability to foresee the likely outcome of a situation is hard to define but easier to identify. One knows foresight when one experiences it. Foresight is a characteristic that enables the servant leader to understand the lessons from the past, the realities of the present, and the likely consequence of a decision for the future. It is also deeply rooted within the intuitive mind. Foresight remains a largely unexplored area in leadership studies, but one most deserving of careful attention.

Servant leadership, like stewardship, assumes first and foremost a commitment to serving the needs of others. It also emphasizes the use of openness and persuasion, rather than control.

Commitment to the Growth of People

Servant leaders believe that people have an intrinsic value beyond their tangible contributions as workers. As such, the servant leader is deeply committed to the growth of each and every individual within his or her organization. The servant leader recognizes the tremendous responsibility to do everything in his or her power to nurture the personal and professional growth of employees and colleagues. In practice, this can include (but is not limited to) concrete actions such as making funds available for personal and professional development, taking a personal interest in the ideas and suggestions from everyone, encouraging worker involvement in decision-making, and actively assisting laid-off employees to find other positions.

Building Community

The servant leader senses that much has been lost in recent human history as a result of the shift from local communities to large institutions as the primary shaper of human lives. This awareness causes the servant leader to seek to identify some means for building community among those who work within a given institution. Servant leadership suggests that true community can be created among those who work in businesses and other institutions.

Servant leadership characteristics often occur naturally within many individuals, and, like many natural tendencies, they can be enhanced through learning and practise. Servant leadership offers great hope for the future in creating better and more caring institutions.

Chapter 6

Leadership Has A Time Limit

A king's time as ruler rises and falls like the sun.
King Mufasa

Leaders come and go. Positions change. Life is dynamic. Those who do not know this oppress others when they are in power. They forget. Positional power can be intoxicating. People bowing and singing your praises can be enchanting. Mufasa knew this and hence he told his son, Simba, "*A king's time as ruler rises and falls like the sun.*"

Even the sun, as seen from the earth, is not perpetually in one position. Leadership is not for forever. Once there was a monarchy, then the military, afterwards the people ran the affairs of government: They called it democracy.

My mind is drawn to so many African countries that have suffered from unreasonable leaders who took leadership to mean they had a permanent seat of power, often touted as 'president for life'.

I was very young when Zimbabwe attained its independence. It was said to be the golden example of what an African nation with great resources could become. Sadly, having the despot, Robert Mugabe, at its helm for 37 years totally destroyed this resource-rich southern African nation and took away so much from its people. Likewise, Félix Houphouët-Boigny was the first President of Ivory Coast (1960 to 1993), serving for more than three decades until his death. By the same token, Daniel Toroitich arap Moi was a Kenyan statesman and politician who served as the second and longest President of Kenya from 1978 to 2002. Initially, he was acting president by virtue of his having been the vice-president when Mzee Jomo Kenyatta, the nation's founding president died. Ironically, he ruled longer than Jomo Kenyatta did and in the process, set that East African nation back in terms of development, fanning tribal discord that eventually saw the country burning during the infamous 2007-2008 elections.

Normally, successful people are highly committed to their work. Here is the problem: the more committed we are to a given path the harder it is for us to admit when it's time to leave. This is why leaders need term limits – it is often just too difficult for them to set these for themselves.

The three leaders I mentioned above did some pretty good things for their countries. However, there came a time when it would have been prudent for them to leave. Why didn't they leave when it was time to go? Because it is incredibly difficult for highly successful leaders, who have put their heart and soul into something, to look into the mirror and say, "This doesn't work. It's time to go." The very fact that they are so highly committed to what they are doing makes it very hard for them to hear contrary information. This is true for leaders at all levels, be they presidents of countries or CEOs of companies.

I do make one exception, however, and that is with regard to Rwanda's Paul Kagame. His leadership has been, like King Mufasa's, focused on his people rather than his personal interests. In my opinion, two short terms of four years each would not have served the East African nation well. He pulled his country back from the devastation of the genocide; guided them through the recovery years so successfully that one can truly say the nation has healed tremendously and led his people into an economic sphere that has won the admiration of the world and all within just two and a half decades.

I have great admiration for this tall, distinguished and charismatic man who brought his country from the brink of extinction and turned around her fortunes. Today, many accolades have changed Rwanda's image from the country that suffered one of the worst genocides in living memory.

In 2018, Kagame who was the head of the African Union (AU) was adjudged the 2018 African of the Year at the eighth All Africa Business Leaders Awards (AABLA). When asked who he was dedicating the award to, his answer was, "The people of Rwanda".

Here is an excerpt from a question and answer by Forbes magazine that clearly shows the positive mindset of this great African leader:

Question: *You are a leader who looks to the future not forgetting a painful past. How hard were the last two decades for you?*

Answer: *Very hard (laughs), which is an understatement, but that is the spirit, about learning lessons of the difficulties you have gone through but not allowing that to hold you back, to make you a hostage of that tragic experience, but rather learn lessons as quickly as you can and focus on where we are going in the future and doing our best to even keep making references to that past if you will. And therefore, helping you to decide which choices to make at any given time in the future. So, 20 years has been a journey of difficulties, but I think of the good stories too, and that is what encourages all of us.*

We have had tragedies, and at the same time, the efforts of bringing people together through reconciliation, through deciding which direction we take for our future… the people have responded with energy, with positivity, and that has not come to nothing, it has actually borne fruit. We've seen progress.

Even the people, when you look at their faces and you look at how they go about things, it's as if nothing ever happened here, yet history is loaded with terrible experiences. And apart from those tragic experiences, we have had other external pressures – people who are quick to forget. Sometimes, the demands [are] even from the outside about how we should deal with things, what we should do, what we shouldn't do, as if our lives are to be decided from the outside and as if we have nothing to do with determining our own course in the future.

But we have calmly had dialogue with such people behind those pressures. We have also focused and really concentrated on what we understand, even the hard choices we have to make, but the good thing is, every three or five years down the road, we were able to measure and say, 'well, what have we gained from the different choices and efforts we made'. Could we have done things differently or even better? Even putting into account all these unnecessary external lessons, and pressures, we still listen. We don't fall short on that. We always listen, but at the same time, we fully understand we are the ones for ourselves.

Mufasa's message about leadership having an expiry on it is totally in keeping with African indigenous leadership.

The accountability of leaders was reinforced because there were many possible candidates for leadership, so strict criteria were applied to determine who would emerge as a leader. To emerge as a leader, candidates had to show competence in:

- understanding people and human nature
- understanding human relationships, conflicts and how to manage them
- diplomacy and relationships with other kingdoms
- the art of war
- strategic thinking; and
- kingdom secrets and how to guard them.

African leadership was much more participatory than appears from the outside. Nelson Mandela describes the profound influence that the democratic decision-making processes of the Thembu people (of which his grandfather was chief) had on him: "*Everyone who wanted to speak could do so. It was democracy in its purest sense. There may have been a hierarchy of importance amongst the speakers, but everyone was heard. Only at the end of the meeting as the sun was setting would the regent speak. His purpose was to sum up what had been said and form some consensus among the diverse opinions. But no conclusion was forced on those who disagreed.*"

While the king was the most visible leader and the indigenous custodian of power, auxiliary authorities — often people of highly respected religious or elder status — continually advised the king in roles that promoted democracy in the kingdom. A study of African leadership and literature indicates that while the king or queen generally appeared very powerful from outside, he or she was nevertheless subject to very strict control, not only by means of taboos but also from institutions and personalities whose main occupation was the protection and safeguarding of the people, the ancestors, the land and the unborn.

Indigenous leadership, therefore, was not comprised solely of the authority of the ruler but was influenced by queen mothers, godfathers, councils, secret societies, mystics, rituals, ceremonies, rules and citizens. The king's decisions and policies were continually subject to review by others. Among the Bantus, a council of elders often played a key governance role in the kingdom in the following ways:

Custodianship of the kingdom. The elders were concerned with the welfare of the land, the living, the ancestors and the unborn. Individual chiefs or kings could come and go but the council was a permanent structure.

Advising the king. The king would use the council as a sounding board for his ideas and critical issues facing the kingdom. For example, on the occasion of identifying his or her successor, the chief would propose the name to the council who would discuss the issue and give their feedback.

Managing conflicts and disputes on behalf of the king in courts. The chief only listened while the council dealt with the cases. After a case was concluded, the council would meet with the king or queen to give them their view. The chief would examine it against what he had heard. They then would come up with a joint stand and the chief would announce the judgement.

Managing the transition from one king to the next. The council had to approve an identified candidate and mentor and coach them. If the king died suddenly, the council managed the transition to the next king by putting in place an interim ruler while initiating a process to identify the permanent ruler.

All of the above simply go to re-emphasize that leadership is not something that just happens like weeds growing unabated. No, like any crop that is expected to bear good fruit, its seeds are carefully chosen, the land prepared carefully, the seeds once planted are tended to carefully through every season and when the time comes for harvest, the effort and care are deemed to have been worthwhile.

Chapter 7

Women's Brand of Leadership

Where women rule, streams run uphill.
Ethiopian proverb

Women managers who have broken the glass ceiling in medium-sized, nontraditional organizations have proven that effective leaders don't come from one mould. They have demonstrated that using the command-and-control style of managing others, a style generally associated with men in large traditional organizations, is not the only way to succeed.

The first female executives, because they were breaking new ground, adhered to many of the "rules of conduct" that spelt success for men. Now a second wave of women is making its way into top management, not by adopting the style and habits that have proved successful for men but by drawing on the skills and attitudes they developed from their shared experience as women. These second-generation managerial women are drawing on what is unique to their socialization as women and creating a different path to the top. They are seeking and finding opportunities in fast-changing and growing organizations to show that they can achieve results—in a different way. They are succeeding because of—not in spite of—certain characteristics generally considered to be "feminine" and inappropriate in leaders.

The women's success shows that a non-traditional leadership style is well suited to the conditions of some work environments and can increase an organization's chances of surviving in an uncertain world. It supports the belief that there is strength in a diversity of leadership styles.

Although there is a great deal of public interest in ensuring more women become leaders, thereby reversing their under-representation in the ranks of power, too many suggested solutions are founded on the misconception that women ought to emulate men. The thinking is: "If men have most of the top roles, they must be doing something right, so why not get women to act like them?"

But this logic fails to account for the relatively dismal performance of most leaders — who are overwhelmingly male. As we have argued before, the real problem is not a lack of competent females; it is too few obstacles for incompetent males, which explains the surplus of overconfident, narcissistic, and unethical people in charge.

As a consequence, gender differences in leadership effectiveness (what it takes to perform well) are out of sync with gender differences in leadership emergence (what it takes to make it to the top). Indeed, research shows that the prevalence of male senior leaders is not a product of superior leadership talent in men. Rather, large quantitative studies, including meta-analyses, indicate that gender differences in leadership talent are either non-existent, or they actually favour women.

With this in mind, it would be more logical to flip the suggested remedy: instead of encouraging women to act like male leaders (many of whom are incompetent), we should be asking men in power to adopt some of the more effective leadership characteristics more commonly found in women. This would create a pool of better role models who could pave the way for both competent men and women to advance.

Motivate through transformation. Academic studies show that women are more likely to lead through inspiration, transforming people's attitudes and beliefs, and aligning people with meaning and purpose (rather than through carrots and sticks), than men are. Since transformational leadership is linked to higher levels of team engagement, performance, and productivity, it is a critical path to improving leaders' performance. If men spent more time trying to win people's hearts and souls, leading with both EQ and IQ, as opposed to leaning more on the latter, and nurturing a change in beliefs rather than behaviour, they would be better leaders.

Put your people ahead of yourself

It's very hard to turn a group of people into a high-performing team when your main focus is yourself. People who see leadership as a glorified career destination and individual accomplishment are too self-centered to foster their teams' wellbeing and unlock their subordinates' potential. Imagine a person who is only interested in being a leader because they are chasing a bigger paycheck, the corner office, a more senior title, or any form of status. Clearly, they will be inherently less interested in making others better; their only goal is to be more successful themselves. Because men are generally more self-focused than women, they are more likely to lead in a narcissistic and selfish way. If the average male leader wants to improve their performance, they would do well to adopt a less self-centered style of leadership.

Don't command; empathize

Throughout history, we have told women that they are too kind and caring to be leaders, but the notion that someone who is not kind and caring can lead effectively is at odds with reality. We are not living in medieval times. Twenty-first-century leadership demands that leaders establish an emotional connection with their followers, and that is arguably the only reason to expect leaders to avoid automation. Indeed, while AI will hijack the technical and hard-skill elements of leadership, so long as we have humans at work, they will crave the validation, appreciation, and empathy that only humans — not machines — can provide. Men can learn a lot about how to do this effectively by watching and emulating women.

Focus on elevating others

Female leaders have proven more likely to coach, mentor, and develop their direct reports than male leaders. They are true talent agents, using feedback and direction to help people grow. This means being less transactional and more strategic in their relationship with employees, and it also includes the openness to hire people who are better than themselves, because their egos are less likely to stand in the way. This enables them to unlock other people's potential and promote effective cooperation on their teams. While we gravitate towards leaders who are self-focused and self-centered, the likelihood that such individuals can turn a group of people into a high-performing team is low.

Don't say you're "humbled." Be humble.

We have been asking for humble leaders for 20 years or so, but we keep gravitating toward ones who are overconfident and narcissistic (generally not female). There are well-established gender differences in humility, and they favour women. Not all women are humble, of course, but selecting leaders on humility would result in more female than male leaders. Humility is fundamentally a feminine trait. It is also one that is essential to being a great leader. Without humility, it will be very hard for anyone in charge to acknowledge their mistakes, learn from experience, take into account other people's perspectives, and be willing to change and get better. Perhaps the issue is not that men are unwilling or unable to display it, but that we dismiss them for leadership roles when they do. This must change, for humility is a critical driver of leadership effectiveness in both men and women.

The COVID-19 crisis points to female leadership as a marker for healthier and more equal societies that are more receptive to political agendas placing social and environmental wellbeing at the core of national policymaking, according to a new analysis involving Lorenzo Fioramonti from the University of Pretoria and Luca Coscieme from Trinity.

The researchers ran some statistical analyses on available COVID-19 pandemic data and a series of dimensions of basic human needs, inequality and economic resilience. For the analyses, they used continuous daily data of the number of confirmed COVID-19 deaths for a total of 35 countries from December 31st, 2019 to May 11th, 2020 (data is available from the European Centre for Disease Prevention and Control).

They reported a summary of some of the stunning correlations, which include:

Countries with women in position of leadership suffered six times fewer confirmed deaths from COVID-19 than countries with governments led by men. Female-led governments were more effective and rapid at flattening the epidemic's curve, with peaks in daily deaths roughly six times lower than in countries ruled by men.

The average number of days with confirmed deaths was 34 in countries ruled by women and 48 in countries ruled by men. Luca Coscieme, Marie Skodowska-Curie and Irish Research Council Fellow, in Trinity College Dublin's School of Natural Sciences, is one of the authors of the study. He said, "Female-led governments shared similar approaches to the crisis, characterized by early consultation with national health experts and advisors, and containment measures were implemented early. On the other hand, most male-led governments downplayed initial warnings and acted with substantial delays to respond to the crisis."

For example, while on March 14 (with only 102 confirmed cases of coronavirus) the New Zealand's government led by Jacinda Ardern announced stringent lockdown and quarantine measures, at a similar time the UK government led by Boris Johnson allowed on March 10 to 13 (with over 700 confirmed cases), the gathering of many thousands of people at large events such as UEFA Champions League soccer fixtures, the Cheltenham Festival, Crufts, and music gigs.

A similarly positive pattern occurred in Denmark, Norway and Finland, all ruled by women, as opposed to Sweden, ruled by a man, where economic considerations trumped health concerns, and ultimately resulted in the highest death toll per capita in Europe.

The authors of the study added:

"Over the past few years, most women-led governments have also placed a stronger emphasis on social and environmental wellbeing, investing more in public health and reducing air pollution—which seems to be closely associated with COVID-19 deaths. Our analysis shows that countries with women-led governments better deliver on Basic Human Needs, one component of the Social Progress Index, which considers aspects of basic medical care, sanitation, shelter and personal safety."

Income distribution and economic recovery

Other key results from the analysis include the finding that countries with women leaders tend to be more equal, with, on average, a 5-point lower Gini Index of income distribution than countries with male leaders.

With regards to resilience and recovery after the crisis, the results show that women-led countries are likely to suffer the least from the ensuing economic recession: GDP growth forecasts for 2020 indicate that they will experience a decline less than 5.5%, while countries with male leaders will shrink by over 7%.

Some of these women-led governments have recently launched an international alliance to promote 'social and ecological wellbeing' as the cornerstone of their economic policies.

The authors said:

"There is evidence for women to more likely take up positions of leadership in societies that value equity, solidarity and collaboration, which are usually associated

with healthier communities. As the risk of pandemics and vector-borne diseases increases, we might want to reconsider what is good policymaking, and what policies make our economies and societies resilient to shocks."

Let's go on a slightly different path into history and look at women in Africa's political struggle.

There were many women who made an indelible mark in the political struggles of various African countries. Let's see who they were that we might celebrate them and learn from their stories.

Ransome-Kuti

When the British colonial officers refused to give permits for demonstrations, activist Funmilayo Ransome-Kuti mobilized local market women for what she called "picnics" and festivals.

One of few women in early 1920s Nigeria to receive post-primary education, Ransome-Kuti used her privilege to coordinate the resistance against colonialism in Nigeria that not only targeted the British but also the local traditional figureheads they used to enforce their rules.

The Abeokuta Women's Union, which she founded, protested unjust taxes, corruption and the lack of women's representation in decision-making corridors. While she is probably better known now as the mother of the Afrobeat pioneer Fela Kuti (an activist in his own right), Ransome-Kuti's role and years as the mother of anti-colonial activism in Nigeria are rarely celebrated outside of early primary school texts. Her son once sang: *"She's the only mother of Nigeria."*

In many ways, the muted legacy of Funmilayo Ransome-Kuti in Nigeria's independence movement plays out across the continent.

In the six decades since many African countries attained political independence, the stories of women in the liberation struggle are yet to be told and celebrated, unlike their male counterparts who wasted no time in having universities, airports and major highways named after them and affixing their faces on national currencies.

For those whose stories have been told, such as anti-apartheid activist Winnie Madikizela-Mandela, they are riddled with double standards and sexist tropes which often try to position them as "helpers" to men and reduce them to wives.

Women, both educated and uneducated, were pivotal to liberation parties, although they were often pigeonholed with the less powerful women's wing of the party if it had one. While they had little opportunity to be part of the broader organogram of these parties, leaders of the women's wing were able to demonstrate enormous leadership potential.

Within a year of being recruited, Bibi Titi Mohammed, as head of the Tanganyika African National Union (TANU) women's wing, had attracted 5,000 women to join. Bibi Titi used women's cultural and economic network to mobilize, exchange information, sell party membership cards, announce rallies, organize marches, and raise money for TANU, which would go on to become the freedom party of modern Tanzania.

In Ghana, Mabel Dove-Danquah, described as a 'trail-blazing feminist' was well ahead of her time as an outspoken advocate for women's equality. Dove-Danquah worked as a writer, journalist and editor for various liberation-minded newspapers including the Accra Evening News which was founded by Kwame Nkrumah. She was among a host of women Nkrumah and his Convention People's Party used to advance the struggle for independence and would go on to become the first African woman to be elected by popular vote to parliament in 1954.

The CPP's women's wing was made up largely of market women who, while criss-crossing the country to buy and sell, went along with the gospel of self-determination. Just like in other African struggles, market women were also the financial backbone of the party but as Ghana commemorated 62 years of independence this month, their names and contributions have effectively been written out of popular history.

In contexts where the fight for independence took a particularly violent turn, women were also on the front lines. Young Muslim women were a central part of the FRELIMO resistance against Portuguese colonial rule in Mozambique. FRELIMO recruited teenage girls and young women as guerrilla fighters and crucially in intelligence gathering as they were seen by the Portuguese as non-threatening. They also performed domestic duties such as cooking and cleaning.

But the lack of recognition for the role of women in history telling is not unique to Africa. Around the world, there have been attempts to rewrite the past and make it fuller and nuanced, says professor Akosua Darkwah, head of the department of sociology at the University of Ghana. *"Often because, these stories are being told by men so they tell it from their perspective,"* she says, *"but there has to be a constant reminder that it couldn't have been that all the women were just sitting down watching."* In 2017,

Darkwah co-authored a paper about women and post-independence African politics.

In struggle times, the leaders of African liberation spoke passionately about women's equality and recognized their contributions. By Nkrumah's own admission: *"much of the success of the CPP has been due to efforts of women members. From the very beginning, women have been the chief field organizers. They have travelled through innumerable towns and villages in the role of propaganda secretaries and have been responsible for the most in bringing about the solidarity and cohesion of the party."*

But that progressive rhetoric was at best a veneer as they did little post-independence to structurally include women in governance and remove sexist colonial-era laws. Although his government introduced a gender quota (9%) [pdf p.3] in the legislature in 1960, Kwame Nkrumah's cabinet as head of government and president, for example, was exclusively male for 11 out of the 14 years he governed. As the economy of newly independent Ghana found itself in dire straits, due to decades of colonialism, the Cold War and his bankrolling of other liberation movements, Nkrumah, picked on market women as a cause of the economic challenges.

Again, women were not spared the brutalities that accompanied criticism of the authoritarian governments that ruled in post-independence Africa. Shortly after independence, Bibi Titi was arrested by the government of her former ally, Julius Nyerere, on trumped-up treason charges. She was sentenced to life in prison but was released after two years on pardon and she spent the rest of her life out of public view.

Similarly, Malawi's first female lawyer Vera Chirwa endured exile and long years of imprisonment when she, along with others, fell out with President Hastings Kamuzu Banda. Chirwa is a founding member of the Malawi Congress Party, which eventually led the country to win independence. She also founded the League of Malawian Women which did not only fight for the rights of women but was a leading supporter of the resistance against white domination in Malawi.

Generations later, the power that women's wings of political parties across the continent wielded have been decimated and usurped by first ladies. They have been depopulated of charismatic, educated, professional women to the extent that a coherent progressive feminist agenda can now be found with civil society. For example, the women's league of the African National Congress (which has been described as "the gatekeepers of patriarchy") until 2017 maintained South Africa was not ready for a woman president, despite the party possessing a cadre of accomplished women politicians.

One of my favourite women leaders is South Africa's Sofia Theresa Williams-de Bruyn. Born in 1938, Sofia is a former South African anti-apartheid activist. On August 9, 1956, she led the march of 20,000 women to the Union Buildings of Pretoria along with Lilian Ngoyi, Rahima Moosa, Helen Joseph, Albertina Sisulu and Bertha Gxowa to protest the requirement that women carry passbooks as part of the pass laws. Sophia was only 18 years old, making her the youngest of the four leaders. These women ducked through the guards at the doors to deliver their petitions outside the ministers' doors. She joined her husband who was already in exile in Zambia, serving in the ANC's military wing. For over 20 years she and her family lived in exile and came back after the ANC and other political parties were unbanned.

There are many untold stories of women's role in the resistance against European colonialism from the women at the frontlines in Algeria and Zimbabwe to the Somali women poets whose words captivated and inspired their freedom movement. However, a new generation of African feminists are determined to reclaim these narratives. They include:

Aya Chebbi

Ms Aya Chebbi is an award-winning Pan-African feminist. She is the first-ever African Union Special Envoy on Youth and the youngest diplomat at the African Union Commission Chairperson's Cabinet. She rose to prominence as a voice for democracy and shot to global fame as a political blogger during 2010/2011 Tunisia's Revolution. She recently received the 2019 Gates Foundation Campaign Award. She is graduate of University of Tunis El Manar with Bachelor in International Relations, Fulbright scholar at George Southern University and Mo Ibrahim Foundation Scholar for her Masters in African Politics at SOAS, University of London.

She is the founder of multiple platforms such as Afrika Youth Movement (AYM), one of Africa's largest Pan-African youth-led movements, Afresist, a youth leadership program and multimedia platform documenting youth work in Africa and Youth Programme of Holistic Empowerment Mentoring (Y-PHEM) coaching the next generation to be positive change agents.

She served on the Board of Directors of CIVICUS World Alliance for Citizen Participation as well as the youngest councilor at the World

Refugee Council and youngest commissioner at Oxfam Independent Commission on Sexual Misconduct.

Her political blogs at Proudly Tunisian were published at Open Democracy and Al-Jazeera, among others. Since then, she has been travelling across the African continent to support and train thousands of social movement leaders and activists on mobilization, blogging, leadership and non-violence and continues to travel the world as a scholar, mentor, speaker and activist.

She was recognized in 2019 Inaugural List of 100 Most Influential African Women, 2019 Most Influential People of African Descent in the Politics & Governance, 2018 Apolitical World's 100 Most Influential Young People in Government and 2016 among 100 Most Influential Young Africans in the World.

Purity Kagwiria
Purity serves as the Executive Director of the Akili Dada Institute, an organization that provides education and leadership opportunity to girls and women in Kenya. A journalist by profession, Purity is an active member of the feminist/women's rights movement and she is committed to analyzing the private and personal spaces that women inhabit and developing strategies that lead to the emancipation of women. Purity holds a degree in Gender and Development from the University of Nairobi and a Diploma in Journalism from Kenya Institute of Mass Communication.

Yaba Badoe
Yaba is a Ghanaian-British documentary filmmaker, producer, and writer. A graduate of King's College in Cambridge, she worked as a

civil servant in Ghana before becoming a General Trainee with the BBC. She has taught in Spain and Jamaica, and has worked as a producer and director making documentaries for the main terrestrial channels in Britain and the University of Ghana in Accra. Her documentaries include The Witches of Gambaga (2011) and The Art of Ama Ata Aidoo (2014).

Maame Afon Yelbert-Obeng

Born and raised in Ghana, Maame is a committed advocate and a passionate leader, who is also a dynamic singer and recording artist. She recently released her second album, titled Ekome. She has worked as a Program Officer for Sub-Saharan Africa (SSA) at the Global Fund for Women, and is a board member and co-chair of the Bay Area Regional Advisory Committee for the African Women's Development Fund in the U.S.A. (AWDF-USA). Maame is also a board member and Program Director for Moremi Initiative for Women's Leadership in Africa, and is also a board member of We Care Solar, an award-winning organization using solar technology to facilitate timely and appropriate emergency care for maternal and infant health.

Leadership comes naturally to African Women

African women have also been influencing national gender policies for over half a century. In 1960, for example, Mail's Jacqueline Ki-zerbo had already developed the idea of considering the gender impacts of policies. It was only decades later that this idea – now commonly known as "gender mainstreaming" – gained international currency, particularly in national budgetary processes.

In key UN conferences, African women activists have been visible from the outset. Egypt's Aida Gindy held the first international meeting on Women in Economic Development in 1972. The Kenya Women's Group helped organise the 1985 UN Conference on Women in which African women brought issues of apartheid and national liberation to the fore. And Egypt's Aziza Husayn helped organise the 1994 Cairo International Conference on Population and Development, which shifted the debate around population control away from a traditional family planning emphasis on quotas and targets to one focused on women's rights and health.

Additionally, Sierra Leone's Filomena Steady was one of the key conveners of the Earth Summit in 1992. Tanzania's Gertrude Mongella was General Secretary of the pivotal 1995 UN Beijing Conference. And African women peace-builders played a crucial role in the 2000 Windhoek conference, which paved the way for a UN Security Council Resolution encouraging the inclusion of women in peace negotiations and peacekeeping missions around the world.

Leading the world

Women in Africa have also set new standards for women's political leadership globally. Women such as Guinea's Jeanne Martin Cissé, Liberia's Angie Brooks and Tanzania's Anna Tibaijuka and Asha-Rose Migiro have all held top positions at the UN. Meanwhile, at a national level, many African countries have made important gains in women's representation.

Rwandan women today hold 62% of the country's legislative seats, the highest in the world. In Senegal, South Africa, Namibia, and Mozambique, more than 40% of parliamentary seats are held by women. There are female speakers of the house in one-fifth of African parliaments, higher than the world average of 14%. Women have claimed positions in key ministries throughout Africa. And women have increasingly run for executive positions, with Liberia, the Central African Republic, Malawi and Mauritius all having had female heads of state. Moreover, these increases in female representation are taking place across the continent, including predominantly Muslim countries such as Senegal, where women hold 43% of legislative seats.

These new patterns are found at the regional level too, with women holding 50% of the positions at the African Union Commission, compared to just one-third at the European Commission. South Africa's Nkosazana Dlamini-Zuma meanwhile chaired the AU Commission from 2012 to 2017.

Women's strong presence in African parliaments has resulted in new discussions about strategies to enhance female political representation worldwide. Scandinavian scholars such as Drude Dahlerup and Lenita Freidenvall even argue that the incremental model that led to high rates of female representation in Nordic countries in the 1970s has now been replaced by the "fast track" African model in which dramatic jumps in representation are brought about by electoral quotas.

Shaping the world

African women have also been pioneering in business. Aspiring young female entrepreneurs today have several role models they can follow such as Ghana's Esther Ocloo, who pursued the idea of formalizing local women's credit associations and became a founding member of one of the first microcredit banks, Women's Worlds Banking, in 1979.

According to the Global Entrepreneurship Monitor, African countries have almost equal numbers of men and women either actively involved in business start-ups or in the phase of starting a new firm. And in countries such as Ghana, Nigeria and Zambia, women are reportedly more likely to be entrepreneurs than men. In fact, Sub-Saharan Africa is the only region in the world where there are more women who become entrepreneurs than men. Women-owned businesses can deliver attractive returns for investors

One of the biggest misconceptions about gender-lens investing is that it is a fad that is more about a feminine revolution than a real business opportunity with competitive returns.

The business case for investing in women entrepreneurs has been researched extensively and it has been proven that women-owned and led businesses can be as competitive as those run by men. They even outperform them in certain industries such as tourism which is key to Africa's development. Companies with gender-diverse leadership also perform better than those with homogeneous management teams.

Women-owned businesses have been found to outlive male-owned enterprises in many industries and research indicates that women tend to be better at risk assimilation. This risk assimilation has been negatively misrepresented as women just being more risk-averse, as if there is something wrong with making a sober assessment of the risks facing a business. A healthy dose of risk aversion and risk-taking is important for a company to thrive.

When it comes to business strategy, women often create strategies that are more holistic and encompassing of both financial and socio-cultural realities. Culture eats strategy for breakfast, so any kind of strategy that does not fully consider and encompass local social and cultural factors is bound to encounter massive challenges when taken to market.

The playing field is not level

Small businesses in Africa already have a hard time securing financing but this funding gap is more pronounced when it comes to women entrepreneurs. This gap exists at various levels of entrepreneurial funding – including bank loans, angel investment, venture capital and private equity – despite there being more women entrepreneurs in sub-Saharan Africa than men.

One of the reasons why many women entrepreneurs are neglected by venture capital investors is because of the industry's focus on technology companies, which have been traditionally male-dominated. Tech has not attracted nor retained women entrepreneurs and while that seems to be shifting, it remains a slow transformation. Limiting funds to male-dominated industries exacerbates this funding gap for women.

Across all levels, women entrepreneurs face social and cultural challenges in Africa which are stifling the growth of their businesses. At a personal level, women in Africa are still expected to be the primary homemakers and childcare providers. They face hurdles – such as insufficient support from their partners and other structures – in managing the dual roles of entrepreneur and mother.

In several African countries, business is predominantly viewed as a man's domain and women tend not to be taken seriously and may face hostility. However, according to The Global Entrepreneurship Monitor, Africa now has the highest growth in businesses started and run by women. In many fields, women entrepreneurs are leading the way.

Here are some examples of women entrepreneurs that are great business leadership models:

Zeenat Ghoor

After studying civil engineering at UCT, Zeenat Ghoor gained experience across the spectrum of civil and structural engineering projects.

Undaunted by the challenges of operating in a traditionally male-dominated industry, Ghoor started her own construction and consulting engineering practice. Working primarily with skilled disadvantaged artisans, she began by doing new builds and renovations for homeowners. Today, the company attracts projects worth hundreds of millions.

Dineo Lioma

Not yet 30 years old, Dineo Lioma has already co-founded three innovative companies in the biotechnology sphere.

In cooperation with IBM, Deep Medical Therapeutics is working on artificial intelligence (AI) systems for helping doctors determine the best therapies for drug-resistant diseases, like TB. Cape Biotechnologies manufactures laboratory reagent enzymes for use in molecular biology research. While Incitech is developing a device for faster diagnosis of HIV.

Dineo has been chosen as one of Forbes Africa's Top 20 Wealth Creators.

Fatuma Namutosi

Fatuma is a director at Byeffe Foods Ltd based in Mbale, Uganda. She was raised by a single mother who funded her education through agriculture. Namutosi through her mother, derived a passion for agriculture and founded Byeffe Foods in 2015.

It produces nutritious food products mainly from pumpkin for pregnant women and infants who are over 6 months old. Namutosi currently employs 1,280 youth of which 70 per cent are female.

Sheila Alumo

Sheila, CEO and founder of Eastern Agricultural Development Company based in Soroti, Uganda, speaks with optimism about how her business has managed to improve the nutrition of the consumers while also enhancing the livelihoods of the smallholder farmers with whom they partner.

"In the areas that we are working in Teso and Karamoja region for instance, malnutrition is at its highest, poverty is at its highest. So, our approach generally is a market systems-based approach; we produce, promote, process and package health and nutrition goods for consumption but while we are doing this, we are creating sustainable business opportunities for about 3,500 rural smallholder farmers," she said.

Alumo also emphasizes that while her workforce is female-dominated, they aim to improve the livelihoods of both male and females smallholder farmers because it takes both to make a family and that a joint effort would be more effective in effecting a transformation.

Proudly and authentically Nigerian

Nigeria is the leading economy in Africa right now and an exciting place to be a woman entrepreneur. I am proud to showcase some of the inspirational women entrepreneurs who are changing the face of business in the country and getting the world to sit up and take notice of the products they are creating and the business empires they are building. Each of these businesswomen, in their own unique way, is flying the flag for Nigeria, either at home or around the world.

Tara Fela-Durotoye

Take a look at this Nigerian-born lawyer turned Africa's leading beauty and makeup entrepreneur. She started House of Tara at the age of 20, from her living room, whilst an undergraduate at university back in 1998. She's since gone on to launch Nigeria's first-ever bridal directory in 1999, and in 2004 she opened the country's leading beauty academy. Today, Tara has over 3,000 reps spread across Nigeria and 14 stores to her name and she is steadfastly dedicated to realizing her vision of building a globally respected beauty company of African origin. Tara remains an inspirational role-model and mentor to make-up artists and aspiring beauty business owners across Africa.

In 2013, Tara was nominated as a Young Global Leader by the World Economic Forum and was also named one of Forbes '20 Young Power African Women'.

This is a great story of a true African brand builder that is not only changing the face of an entire industry sector in her country but is also empowering and training a new generation of young women entrepreneurs to follow in her footsteps and continue her legacy. Tara Fela-Durotoye is an inspiration to all those African women entrepreneurs who have a vision for their own businesses and who also wish to make a positive impact on the lives of others on the continent.

Bethlehem Tilahun Alemu

Bethlehem is founder and Managing Director of soleRebels, the world's fastest-growing African footwear brand and the only Fair Trade-certified footwear company in the world. Growing up in a poor suburb of Addis Ababa, Bethlehem decided that there was only one way to defeat poverty – use local craftsmanship to make products that can compete in the global marketplace. She decided on footwear and today 70,000 pairs of shoes leave her factory every year. soleRebels has been expanding rapidly and has 18 stores around the world, including in Silicon Valley (USA), Japan, Singapore, Austria, Greece, Spain and Switzerland, along with an aggressive e-commerce marketing strategy. It expects to open another 50 to 60 stores in the next 18 to 36 months. In 2015, Bethlehem launched a new venture, Republic of Leather, offering bespoke, handcrafted leatherwear and accessories.

Bethlehem was the first female African entrepreneur to address the Clinton Global Initiative; was named Outstanding African Business Woman by African Business Awards in 2011, and was named one of the top 12 women entrepreneurs of the last century by CNN. Bethlehem is a UN Goodwill Ambassador for Entrepreneurship and also sits on the board of the United Nations Industrial Development Organisation (UNIDO).

From the humblest of beginnings, Bethlehem has built soleRebels into the planet's fastest-growing African footwear brand and the very first global footwear brand to ever emerge from a developing nation. She has created world-class jobs and empowered her community and country, whilst presenting a galvanized, dynamic face of African creativity to the global market.

Bethlehem was born and raised in the Zenabwork/Total area of Addis Ababa, one of the most impoverished and marginalized communities of Ethiopia. Growing up Bethlehem saw that Ethiopia had plenty of charity "brands" but not a single global brand of its own, so she set out to change all that. In early 2005, fresh out of college in Addis Ababa, Bethlehem founded the trailblazing footwear company soleRebels to provide solid community-based jobs. Tapping into her community's and the nation's rich artisan wealth and heritages, Bethlehem started re-imagining what footwear could be.

Seven years, many shoes and hundreds of creative, dignified and well-paying jobs later, soleRebels is the planet's fastest-growing African footwear brand and the world's first and only World Fair Trade Federation [WFTO] Fair Trade certified footwear company. Constantly elevating the idea of what her brand can achieve, Bethlehem has led soleRebels to become the first-ever brand from a developing nation to open branded, stand-alone retail stores around the globe including in Asia and the EU. soleRebels became the first global branded retail chain from a developing nation to open 100 stores and achieve over USD 100 million in revenues by 2017.

Female representation in boardrooms worldwide is very poor, but Africa's rate of 14.4% is only slightly behind Europe (18%) and the US (17%), and ahead of Asia, Latin America and the Middle East.

Finally, a younger generation of activists is emerging throughout Africa today and redefining feminism from an African perspective. One sees this not only in the work of the African Feminist Forum, which first met in 2006, but also in the work of figures such as novelist Chimamanda Ngozi Adichie who issued a clarion call to women in her video We Should All be Feminist, adapted from her 2013 Ted Talk, in which she explores what it means to be an African feminist. Her book-length essay by the same title is found on bookshelves in major cities around the world, and the Swedish Women's Lobby has given it to every 16-year-old in Sweden to help them think about gender equality.

Feminist discourse meanwhile has become commonplace throughout the continent on websites, blogs, journals, and social media. New feminist novels like Dust by Yvonne Adhiambo Owuor (Kenya), Kintu by Jennifer Nansubuga Makumbi (Uganda), and Americanah by Adichie (Nigeria) have offered new ways of imagining women.

There are clearly still enormous hurdles for African feminists to overcome in fighting for gender equality. But as they have over the past half a century, Africa's women activists of today are reshaping not only African feminist agendas in tackling these challenges but global ones as well.

However, there is no question that Africa has forgotten the women leaders of its independence struggle. Let us document our current stories well so that no stories are romanticized, or told in a manner that takes away from those whose sacrifices we are beneficiaries.

Chapter 8

Leadership by The Youth

"… service to humanity is the best work of life."
Junior Chamber International

When I was growing up I constantly heard the words, *"You are the leaders of tomorrow."* My silent response was often this, *"When will tomorrow come? What if tomorrow does not come soon enough or at all?"*

Today, I see many, many TEENS taking action on implementing sustainability solutions, at home and abroad. They do not wait or ask anyone to do something, expect no gratification, do not drop pills, do not drop out, do not reiterate dysfunctional ideological memes, do not hate adults making bad decisions, do not stigmatize groups or define themselves by what they do. They do what needs doing. They ARE the change.

In this chapter, I will look at those institutions that are impacting the youth, and raising leaders among the youth. I will also explore those things that empower and by the same token, those that disempower the youth.

One institution stands out for me and I admire their ethos and the caliber of young leaders that are synonymous with their membership.

Junior Chamber International, commonly referred to as JCI, is a membership-based nonprofit organization of 200,000 young people ages 18 to 40 in 5,000 communities and more than 100 countries around the world. Each JCI Member shares the belief that in order to create lasting positive change, we must improve ourselves and the world around us. We seek targeted solutions to the unique problems in our communities to build a better world, creating global impact.

At the individual level

Activities within JCI are geared toward increasing individual members' personal development and helping them to reach their full potential. Junior Chamber provides members numerous opportunities to develop skills as officers and project leaders of local and national organizations and of communities. To provide members with the best personal and development training. JCI offers many programs as well as certification from its International Training Institute. By helping individual members acquire experience as decision-makers, JCI contributes to the development of tomorrow's community and business leaders.

The Business Angle

JCI provides its members with the necessary contact, leadership, and personal business growth through numerous forums and programs to develop themselves as young entrepreneurs and business executives. The JCI Business Academy offers members the opportunity to certify their business skills, and is the first worldwide JCI program operated totally from the web. JCI strongly supports business development in all lands as a means to eliminate poverty and human suffering.

The Greater Community

JCI believes its members are an investment in the present and future well-being of their communities. Junior Chamber members agree, strongly endorsing the philosophy, "think locally, act globally." Members and community sponsors alike know that helping their community has an impact on their state or region, that a regional project will benefit their nation, and that works performed on a national level can have a tremendous impact internationally. Affirming the final line of the JCI Creed, "That service to humanity is the best work of life," members plan and carry out tens of thousands of JCI projects each year in thousands of communities, making a positive impact on society.

On an International Scale

In an increasingly interdependent world, members realize the need for international collaboration, tolerance, and peace. JCI offers members numerous opportunities to understand and be involved in global issues. Through international conferences, academies, programs, Twinning (sister-chapter relationships), and business exchange, Junior Chamber enables members to promote goodwill and attain a deeper understanding of the global challenges of tomorrow.

As I continued to seek inspiration about leadership by the youth, I recall a poem by the world-recognized poet, playwright and Pan-Africanist, Micere Mugo, entitled, I took My Son by the Hand.

I took my son
by the hand
felt the warm flow
of young blood
comfort my cold
heart

This way we trekked
five long miles
to attend celebrations
It was
the season of peace.
Away with agitators.
Love and brotherhood juu
Division and hatred chini!
We heard of
selfless sacrifice
Condemned
selfishness
Damned
laziness
Extolled
industry
Celebrated
freedom
Carried bursting fruit baskets
high high high
on elevated haughty heads
Towards sunset
we set out

for home
my son's little warm hand
inside mine
he in his world
me in mine
Mother, he asked
Do we have
matunda ya uhuru
in our hut?
I laughed foolishly

Mother!
Yes son
Do we have
some?
Silence
May I eat one
when we get there?
Move on son
darkness is looming fast
around us.

Micere Githae Mugo (1973)

When I first studied the poem, I came away with the understanding of leadership on so many levels. Let me share some of these with you and in doing so, hopefully ignite your own response.

Here is a mother who was distraught because the future she had hoped to gift her son was lacking in the one thing that was critical, leadership.

Independence was being touted but she knew that it was hollow. She is unable to give credible answers to her son's naïve question, "Do we have matunda ya uhuru in our hut? In other words, has freedom really come for all of us?

In my opinion, this young mother knows that the current leadership or lack of it will impact her young son. He, in turn, so young and naïve has questions that show that leadership is not something that will impact him later, but right now.

The reference to sunset and the darkness looming fast is what Africa has experienced for decades because of lack of leadership. It is time for us to now embrace a new season of great leadership.

I know that we are in a new season of leadership across Africa. The gratifying thing is that Africa's leadership was always led by the youth. If you look at history, our iconic leaders were, themselves, very young when they took up the fight against oppression. Here are some fine examples:

Africa's political history is not complete without appreciating the roles that the youth played in achieving their countries' independence. In the years leading to independence, youths were the driving force behind the nationalist activities that led to the dismantling and eventual overthrow of colonialism and the colonial masters. Despite this, the role of youths in African politics has received less than commensurate attention in studies on democratization.

In Nigeria, the activities of Herbert Macaulay, Nnamdi Azikiwe, Obafemi Awolowo, H.O. Davies, Tafawa Balewa, Ahmadu Bello and Samuel Akintola among many others in their 20s and 30s are legendary. Some of these youths are reputed for the formation of political parties such as the Nigerian Youth Movement (NYM), which was the first political party in Nigeria, the Nigeria National Democratic Party (NNDP), and the National Council of Nigeria and the Cameroons (NCNC). These young Nigerians each used the media to speak against the evils of colonialism and demanded independence. Nnamdi Azikiwe, for instance, was reputed for the use of his newspaper, the West African Pilot.

Through these avenues, they created awareness of the evils that foreign domination posed to the country and, despite various constitutional reforms, these young people demanded independence. Their tenacity and determination eventually saw the country gaining independence from British colonial rule on 1 October 1960.

In the years after independence, particularly during the military era, young people opposed and fought gallantly against the profligacy and high-handedness of the military regimes of Yakubu Gowon and Olusegun Obasanjo, and during the brutal and inglorious regimes of Ibrahim Babangida and Sani Abacha in the 1980s and 1990s, an entire generation of youth and student organisations formed under umbrella organisations such as the National Association of Nigerian Students, the Campaign for Democracy, the Civil Liberties Organisation and the Committee for the Defense of Human Rights. These took the struggle to the streets of major cities across the country.

Stephen Bantu Biko

He was one of the greatest young leaders of South Africa who fought against the apartheid regime in South Africa. In July 1969, Biko was elected as the first president of the South African Students Association (SASO) and in 1970 he was elected as the Chair of SASO Publication and he started publishing articles under the pseudonym Frank Talk, under the heading, I Write What I Like, which eventually became a book. Biko later on quit his medical studies and became fully involved in the Black Community Programmes (BCP) which was an arm of the Black Consciousness Movement (BCM). Biko was banned in 1973 but that didn't restrict the influence of BCM in the political sphere of South Africa.

On August 27, 1976, during the Soweto Uprising, Biko was arrested and put under solitary confinement for 101 days. In 1977 Biko was arrested. He was badly beaten and suffered a brain hemorrhage. The police still kept him chained despite his condition and drove him for 12 hours, naked at the back of a van, on a 700km distance to Pretoria. Biko died on 12 September 1977. Donald Woods, a close friend of Steve said, "In the three years that I grew to know him, my conviction never wavered that this was the most important political leader in the entire country, and quite simply the greatest man I have ever had the privilege to know." Biko died at the age of 30.

Thomas Sankara

Burkina Faso, land of the upright man owes its name to Thomas Isidore Sankara, a revolutionary army Captain who took over power in a coup d'état in 1983. Sankara took radical steps in changing his country's outlook, both in the foreign policies and domestic policies.

His international policies bore anti-imperialist stances, shunning foreign aid and nationalizing all land and mineral wealth. In the domestic front, he led nationwide literacy programs, promoted public health vaccinations of meningitis, measles and yellow fever, banned female genital mutilation (FGM) and appointed women to top positions in the government. His image was a source of inspiration to many. On October 15th, 1987 at the age of 37, he was assassinated by his best friend Blaise Compaore. A week before his assassination he had declared that "While revolutionaries as individuals can be murdered, you cannot kill ideas."

Amilcar Cabral

Though not a Marxist, he was heavily influenced by Marxist ideologies. He founded the Portuguese for African Party for the Independence of Guinea and Cape Verde (PAIGC) in 1956 but launched its first military attack in 1963, claiming lands from the Portuguese and gaining support from the masses.

Fidel Castro said of him, *"one of the most lucid and brilliant leaders in Africa, who instilled in us tremendous confidence in the future and the success of his struggle for liberation."*

Patrick Chabal, a professor of Lusophone studies in his book Amilcar Cabral: Revolutionary Leadership and People's War said,

"In less than twenty years of active political life, Cabral led Guinea-Bissau's nationalists to the most complete political and military success ever achieved by an African political movement against a colonial power. At the time of his death in 1973, months before Guinea-Bissau became independent, his influence extended well beyond the Lusophone world and Africa. Friends and foes alike admired his political acumen and skills and saw in him a potential leader of the non-aligned movement. His writings have shown him to be a sophisticated analyst of the social,

economic and political factors which have affected and continue to affect the developing world."

On January 20, 1973 Amilcar Cabral was assassinated. His famous quote *"Tell no lies, claim no easy victories, tell it to the people the way it is,"* is often reiterated by student union leaders.

Tom Mboya

Thomas Joseph Adhiambo Mboya was a former Minister of Justice and Constitutional Affairs, a trade unionist, Pan Africanist and one of Kenya's founding fathers. He served as a sanitary inspector for the Nairobi City Council and faced racism many times. In his book Freedom and After he said, "A number of times I was physically thrown out of premises which I had gone to inspect by Europeans who insisted they wanted a European, not an African, to do the job. The City Council had to prosecute a number of them for obstructing African inspectors in the course of their duties". At the age of 28, he was elected the chairman of the All-African People's Conference convened by Kwame Nkrumah.

Mboya played a crucial role in establishing the trade unions in Kenya, Tanzania and Uganda and also in creating the 'students' air-lift' which helped many Kenyan students go to the United States for studies. Described as erudite and intelligent, Mboya designed the flag of Kenya and organized various labour union platforms across the continent. While serving as the Minister for Economic Planning and Development, Mboya was assassinated on July 5, 1969 at the age of 38.

The Youth of South Africa

The ultimate picture of youth-led leadership and victory has to be the Soweto Uprising. The June 16, 1976 Uprising that began in Soweto and spread countrywide profoundly changed the socio-political landscape in South Africa. Events that triggered the uprising can be traced back to policies of the Apartheid government that resulted in the introduction of the Bantu Education Act in 1953. The rise of the Black Consciousness Movement (BCM) and the formation of South African Students Organisation (SASO) raised the political consciousness of many students while others joined the wave of anti-Apartheid sentiment within the student community. When the language of Afrikaans alongside English was made compulsory as a medium of instruction in schools in 1974, black students began mobilizing themselves. On 16 June 1976 between 3,000 and 10,000 students mobilized by the South African Students Movement's Action Committee supported by the BCM marched peacefully to demonstrate and protest against the government's directive. The march was meant to culminate at a rally at the Orlando Stadium.

On their pathway, they were met by heavily armed police who fired teargas and later live ammunition on demonstrating students. This resulted in a widespread revolt that turned into an uprising against the government. While the uprising began in Soweto, it spread across the country and carried on until the following year.

The aftermath of the events of June 16th, 1976 had dire consequences for the Apartheid government. Images of the police firing on peacefully demonstrating students led to an international revulsion against South Africa as its brutality was exposed. Meanwhile, the weakened and exiled liberation movements received new recruits fleeing political persecution at home giving impetus to the struggle against Apartheid.

The power of the youth must never be underestimated because it has been the catalyst, the driver and the reason for the struggle for a brighter future for Africa!

One organization that has recognized this is The Mandela Washington Fellowship for Young African Leaders as the flagship program of the U.S. Government's Young African Leaders Initiative (YALI). Since 2014, nearly 4,400 young leaders from every country in Sub-Saharan Africa have participated in the Fellowship. The Fellows, between the ages of 25 and 35, are accomplished leaders and have established records of promoting innovation and positive impact in their communities and countries. In 2020, the Fellowship will provide 700 outstanding young leaders from Sub-Saharan Africa with the opportunity to hone their skills at a U.S. college or university with support for professional development after they return home.

One more institution, the African Leadership Academy, caught my interest a few years ago. Let me share that which I found intriguing and absolutely admirable about their contribution to Africa's leadership.

The Founders' Story

Born in Ghana but having lived and worked in almost 10 countries across Africa, Fred Swaniker was deeply concerned about the extent to which the African continent was suffering as a result of poor leadership. He also discovered that some African parents were paying extremely high school fees to send their children abroad. He envisioned a world-class academic institution on the African continent where the most outstanding young students can develop into leaders who are passionate about the continent and eager to make an impact. Fred shared his concept with friends, among them co-founders Peter Mombaur and Acha Leke, who agreed to provide the initial financial backing.

It wasn't until later when Fred went to Stanford Graduate School of Business where Fred met Chris Bradford that the concept for African Leadership Academy came to fruition. Chris had developed a keen interest in the design of educational institutions, and in their potential to shape societies, and both he and Fred shared a unified dream of transforming a country's leadership landscape by transforming educational systems. They both shared the idea that great leaders come about because of strong institutions, and that in the case of the African continent, those institutions would need to be put in place.

Fred left his job at McKinsey and Chris deferred a number of prestigious full-time job offers to work on ALA full-time. Both Fred and Chris spent nine months working on a pilot version of the Academy's full-time program. Chris led the design of ALA's innovative curriculum, which merges rigorous academics with powerful courses in Entrepreneurial Leadership and African Studies, and shaped the Academy's rigorous and unique admissions process. Fred led ALA's fundraising efforts. In June 2005, Fred and Chris launched the Summer Academy in Cape Town, to pilot ALA's innovative curriculum. The program was a resounding success and bolstered the team's credibility with donors, feeder schools, and potential students and families.

This work was validated in 2006 when Chris and Fred were named Echoing Green Fellows as two of the "leading emerging social entrepreneurs in the world" – selected from over 900 organizations worldwide. Two years later, they opened the doors for ALA's inaugural class in 2008 at their campus in Johannesburg, South Africa.

Their Founding Beliefs:

Address the Underlying Causes of Problems

To create lasting change in Africa, it is necessary to make investments that treat the causes, and not just the symptoms, of under-development in Africa. We believe an undersupply of leadership across all sectors is the root cause of many of Africa's problems. Africa needs strong leaders throughout society, in the spheres of politics, business, health care, education, the environment, and beyond, to create positive change and generate growth and prosperity.

The Power of One

History has seen countless examples of the power of individual leaders to catalyze the actions of large groups of people and unleash massive positive change in society. In South Africa, Nelson Mandela and Desmond Tutu led a peaceful transition from oppression to democracy. Wangari Maathai inspired environmental and political activism by women across Kenya. Bill Gates and Steve Jobs transformed the global economy with their innovations in computing, and Muhammad Yunus created a new path from poverty to prosperity by developing microloans at the Grameen Bank.

The Power of Youth

Many great leaders begin "changing the world" at a young age – when they believe the whole world is open to them and they are free to chase their big dreams. Nelson Mandela was only 26 when he and Walter Sisulu established the ANC Youth League. Bill Gates established

Microsoft at 19, and Steve Jobs launched Apple at age 21. We need to invest in Africa's leaders when they are young and dreaming and give them the confidence they need to bring their ideas to the world.

The Need for Pan-African Cooperation
We believe that a pan-African approach is required to catalyze growth and development in Africa. African leaders must understand and collaborate with peers across the continent to remove barriers to trade, end conflict and stimulate widespread positive change.

Entrepreneurship is Fundamental to Growth
Africa needs entrepreneurial leaders across all sectors who will throw off the constraints of existing institutions to change the paradigm and create value on the continent. Most entrepreneurs in Africa today are "subsistence" entrepreneurs, with small businesses and meagre incomes that allow them to support only their families. To break the cycle of poverty and generate significant growth, however, Africa needs large-scale entrepreneurs.

ALA remains the continent's only pan-African high school, having admitted over 700 students from over 45 African countries to date.

From their website, here is their mission and vision:
"African Leadership Academy, South Africa, seeks to transform Africa by developing a powerful network of over 6,000 leaders who will work together to address Africa's greatest challenges, achieve extraordinary social impact, and accelerate the continent's growth trajectory.

Africa's greatest need is ethical and entrepreneurial leadership. Too often, we only invest in addressing the symptoms of poor leadership in Africa: we give blankets, food, and medicine to those impacted by war, poverty, and famine. But these efforts will never stop unless we develop leaders who prevent wars, entrepreneurs who create jobs, and innovators that develop lasting solutions to the root causes of Africa's problems. We aim to develop the future Nelson Mandela, the next Wangari Maathai…"

The Story of A 25 Year Old Young Entrepreneur From Nigeria

Jerry Isaac Mallo is the chief executive officer of Bennie Technologies LTD. And he made the news within and outside tech circles with the launch of his luxury car. However, here are some important facts to note about the engineer. Jerry was born in Plateau state to Nigerian parents in 1994. He is currently 25 years old and schooled in Nigeria. At least, until he finished his secondary school education. In an interview, the tech genius mentioned that he had always been interested in engineering. He said he wanted to be the Bill Gates of Africa. This could mean both in innovation and wealth. However, he was not from a wealthy family. His opportunity to further his education came after he designed a 'fuel-less generator and proto type car' [sic].

A rich man he called Professor Suleiman Elias Bogoro sponsored his university education after seeing his potential. This gave him the chance to study his dreams at the University of Hertfordshire, London. Sadly, he had to drop out for undisclosed reasons. Although his passion for sports cars didn't drop, he ventured into what he saw as the most lucrative, agriculture. Jerry Mallo Founded Bennie Technologies. His company is named Bennie Technologies LTD and it majorly focuses on agro-technology. Their description on Twitter states: "A machine design, fabrication & manufacturing company. We simplify local agricultural processes by mechanization & automation." It won the National MSME(Micro Small and Medium Enterprise) award in 2018.

The Federal government of Nigeria runs this programme. With the company, he has created many things and has come a long way from the initial tractor he designed. Now they create grinding machines, cassava peelers and many other machines depending on what the customer demands. But as we stated, his sports' car passion never died. And to show this, in November 2019, he launched the HYPERLINK

https://www.plat4om.com/bennie-technologies-ceo-jerry-mallo-unveils-nigeria's-first-luxury-car/Bennie Purrie

Nigeria's first luxury sports car designed with carbon fibre. Mr. Mallo said he chose the 108 material because of its safety quality and not performance. The Bennie Purrie was launched in Abuja. Carbon fibre as he explained in a video absorbs shock better than aluminium and steel. This would reduce fatality in accidents as it won't, unlike the pre-mentioned materials, fold and cause further harm to vehicle occupants. He now adds 'Bennieautomobile' to his Tweets and it looks like he is creating a car company. In the same video, he mentioned that he had recruited young and brilliant minds like himself to help on the Bennie Purrie project. With their success, it is definitely just a matter of time before they start to startle the world with further inventions.

Our Model: Connect to Opportunity

Young leaders are guided by a powerful network along their path to transformative impact in Africa. For instance, Young leader Iman Bermaki from Morocco was able to speak about her aspirations for youth development on the continent at the opening of the annual Mo Ibrahim Forum in Dakar, Senegal. She spoke alongside former Nigerian President Olusegun Obasanjo and co-founder of Africa 2.0, Mamadou Toure.

Our Model: Identify Potential

We comb Africa for youth who show the spark of initiative, who see what can be and strive to make it so. For example, after losing a friend to Cholera, young leader Solomon Martey from Ghana invented a borehole 109 machine using spare parts to pump, purify, and distribute water in his village. His machine has since been adopted by the Ghanaian Ministry of Environment and rolled out in several other rural villages across Ghana. I am sure there are many other institutions across Africa that are preparing our leadership and I applaud each one of them. They are the reason we have hope for a brighter future for this continent.

Our Model: Connect to Opportunity

Young leaders are guided by powerful network along their path to transformative impact in Africa. For instance, Young leader Iman Bermaki from Morocco was able to speak about her aspirations for youth development on the continent at the opening of the annual Mo Ibrahim Forum in Dakar, Senegal. She spoke alongside former Nigerian President Olusegun Obasanjo and co-founder of Africa 2.0, Mamadou Toure.

Our Model: Identify Potential

We comb Africa for youth who show the spark of initiative, who see what can be and strive to make it so. For example, after losing a friend to Cholera, young leader Solomon Martey from Ghana invented a borehole machine using spare parts to pump, purify, and distribute water in his village. His machine has since been adopted by the Ghanaian Ministry of Environment and rolled out in several other rural villages across Ghana.

I am sure there are many other institutions across Africa that are preparing our leadership and I applaud each one of them. They are the reason we have hope for a brighter future for this continent.

Chapter 9

Leadership & The Media

"Social media creates communities, not markets."
Don Schultz, marketing pioneer

The topic of leadership in the media industry is a compelling one. While other industries have leaders or captains, the media sector has moguls, magnates and barons. Randolph Hearst, William Paley, Henry Luce and Robert Maxwell represent some of the most controversial and flamboyant business leaders of recent times. Contemporary media industry leaders such as Rupert Murdoch, Ted Turner and the late Steve Jobs, are not only charismatic, they have made an indelible mark on the industry and the world.

As a leader in media, Ted Turner changed our world, without question. Before CNN, people didn't think that a 24-hour-a-day news channel was viable. How did Ted prove them wrong? His answer:
"It helps to see over the horizon," Ted said, *"most people can't do it, but I think your brain is like a muscle. And just like any other muscle, you can use it and your brain will improve."*

Ted goes on to explain that he knew he was going to have to work hard if he wanted to accomplish something in life,
"So, I read a lot — classics, warfare, Alexander the Great — I used my brain all the time. Everything I did was education. Others just shot the breeze, wasted time — nothing wrong with that, but you can't get to the top doing that."

What did Ted see over the horizon? As Ted described it, the idea for CNN was born of his own desire to stay on top of the news but, as a busy executive, not having time to watch the news during the two times a day it was on during the 1970s. *"I knew I was gambling with CNN, but I knew it would work,"* Ted said. *"At the time, the news came on at 6:30 and again at 11 pm. I never saw the news — it was inconvenient. I knew that having news on 24 hours a day so you could check in any time was something that people would want."*

Beyond CNN, Ted was also working to build a multichannel universe. CNN fitted into this universe perfectly. In the 1970s, three broadcast networks — ABC, NBC and CBS — controlled the programming people could see. For example, sports games across the country were televised, but they couldn't be seen outside the local area because the broadcasters had a monopoly. *"The broadcasters had carved up the games,"* Ted said, dividing the NFL, AFL and Monday Night Football between them. *"Everyone paid the same prices and made the same profit. All three networks were happy, but I wasn't happy"* — customers weren't being served, and incumbents had no incentive to change.

This is where Ted's reading and habit of learning came into play again. *"It was in early 1975 that I saw an article about communications satellites in Broadcasting magazine,"* Ted recalled. Reading the article, Ted realized that he could use one satellite "antenna" in space to cover all of North America. He'd found a way to compete with the established networks.

It is particularly important that the leaders we have controlling aspects of our lives such as the media are ethical persons, people of integrity and wisdom. Of course, to some extent, social media has levelled some of the playing fields and even in that space, we would be looking for leaders and looking to see how social media influences leaders.

In times of deep social and technological change, social media enables leaders to take advantage of the radical cognitive and relational transformations that are taking place everywhere. Social media creates within leaders and through them more capacity to metabolize the complexity of our modern world and turn it into a strategic advantage.

The use of social media is often described as transformative for good reasons. These new channels generate new types of interaction – they create new ways to relate to one another. This is why it is fundamentally experiential and cannot be delegated without dampening its impact.

Social media evolves collective identity from "territory" to "network." This enhances the capacity to welcome diverse input. As a result, culture becomes reflective of more voices and becomes more capable of synchronizing with the complexity of the world to transform disruptions into opportunities.

When some leaders at Sanofi Pasteur, the vaccines division of a multinational pharmaceutical company, decided to get personally involved in an internal online community, the result was the unprecedented improvement of the company's manufacturing quality worldwide. Every week, they interacted directly with the broader employee community on the social network: asking questions, sharing insights, recognizing achievements, "liking" posts... Just a few minutes each week had a huge positive impact on their own perception, their leadership, and the flows of knowledge between employees.

Perhaps it was in the Arab Spring that social media as a tool for change made its greatest impact. Given its powerful impact, it is a tool that leaders should seriously consider understanding in its full import.
Almost immediately after the Arab uprisings began, there was debate over the role and influence of social media in the ouster of Tunisian president Zine El Abidine Ben Ali and the imminent overthrow of Mubarak. In covering what some deemed the Facebook or Twitter revolutions, the media focused heavily on young protesters mobilizing in the streets in political opposition, smartphones in hand. And since then, the violent and sectarian unrest in Syria has brought increased attention to the role of citizen journalism.

Social media indeed played a part in the Arab uprisings. Networks formed online were crucial in organizing a core group of activists, specifically in Egypt. Civil society leaders in Arab countries emphasized the role of "the internet, mobile phones, and social media" in the protests. Additionally, digital media has been used by Arabs to exercise freedom of speech and as a space for civic engagement.

Good leadership mandates that we keep up with the times, that we take up tools that can help us carry out our duties even more effectively. Social media is one of the most powerful tools of our time. However, we must also be conscious of its abuse. We have seen world leaders who are unrestrained in the use of Tweeter making blunders, confusing citizenry and being irresponsible.

Media is, at best of times, an extremely powerful tool to be used cautiously. Indeed, how we use such tools goes to demonstrate our level of maturity as leaders.

Chapter 10

Great leadership is an art

Leadership is the art of achieving progress through the involvement and actions of others.
Anon

This is why great leaders are strong in both leading people and leading for results, while good leaders typically focus their leadership on only one or the other. It is the reason why: Great Leaders Focus on People and Results.

Great leaders combine a leadership mindset and written leadership philosophy with strong people leadership skills and a results-oriented focus.

Successful great leaders apply the skills of adaptability, motivation, coaching, focus, collaboration, decision-making, communications, and personal development to both themselves and the people they lead.

Strong great leaders leverage the emotions of passion, enthusiasm, self-satisfaction, trust, and loyalty to drive creativity, thinking, innovation, energy, and buy-in to strategies, tactics, and activities in pursuit of clearly stated goals and objectives.

This philosophy of leadership is applicable across all organizations and institutions, including publicly listed companies, non-profit entities, social and community groups, educational institutions, and even government departments and ministries.

Great Leaders Drive Results

You may have noticed that we do not refer to the achievement of goals and objectives in this definition. Many factors will impact whether particular goals are achieved or attained. Leadership has the role of ensuring progress towards clearly defined goals and objectives.

The inability to achieve a goal is not necessarily failure. After all, learning from non-achievement of a stated objective is not failure, but rather the gaining of new knowledge. Additionally, even small progress is still progress.

It has often been said that managers do things right while leaders do the right things. There's a great deal of truth in this pithy observation. Especially as our concept of great leadership is applied.

Managers should be responsible for ensuring appropriate implementation of policies, procedures, and processes. Great leaders, in addition to determining and communicating direction, are responsible for people leadership and people development. This includes leadership and development of themselves.

The art of great leadership mandates a positive and future-focus mindset. You will not find many successful leaders who are pessimistic. Nor are those focused solely on short-term results (such as quarterly revenue and profit figures) likely to be successful over the long term.

This does not mean leadership requires wearing rose-coloured glasses or having an unrealistic view that all will become right soon.

Rather, the art of great leadership requires a solid grounding in both understanding the reality of any situation, while simultaneously being able to integrate various viewpoints of reality that they and others hold. This means both understanding the status quo and being able to question the underlining nature of the status quo, and how this is perceived and believed by others.

The thing is: anyone at any level of an organization can be a great leader.

Great leadership is not something reserved for senior management, business owners, and entrepreneurs. Anyone can be a great leader, if only of themselves. One does not need direct reports or to head a multi-functional team to be a great leader. As such, anyone can implement the art of great leadership and the skills of great leadership.

Great Leaders Develop People

The people development aspect of leadership is often overlooked by leaders, especially by those put into leadership positions for the first time, such as new supervisors, frontline managers, and newly appointed sales managers who have been promoted due to high sales performance.

However, all great leaders know that their mission is not to create followers but to create more good leaders for their organizations. They also know they need to continuously develop themselves. This is why people development, including one's own personal development, is a core component of the art of great leadership.

The art of great leadership requires a continuous evaluation of one's own leadership skills, mindset, philosophy, actions, and development.

Understanding the art of great leadership will help prevent you from tripping and falling as you pursue your leadership journey.

Chapter 11

Leadership Through the Visual Arts

Tyler Perry's "beyond you" leadership style is also evident on his movie sets.

The visual arts are art forms such as painting, drawing, printmaking, sculpture, ceramics, photography, video, filmmaking, design, crafts, and architecture.

How Does Art Affect Culture and Society? Art influences society by:
- Changing opinions
- Instilling values and
- Translating experiences across space and time.

Research has shown art affects the fundamental sense of self. That in itself speaks of the need for leaders that influence people through the medium of visual arts.

Painting, sculpture, music, literature and the other arts are often considered to be the repository of a society's collective memory. Art preserves what fact-based historical records cannot: how it felt to exist in a particular place at a particular time.

Art in this sense is communication; it allows people from different cultures and different times to communicate with each other via images, sounds and stories. Art is often a vehicle for social change. It can give voice to the politically or socially disenfranchised. A song, film or novel can rouse emotions in those who encounter it, inspiring them to rally for change.

Art also has utilitarian influences on society. There is a demonstrable, positive correlation between schoolchildren's grades in math and literacy and their involvement with drama or music activities.

Art not only fosters the human need for self-expression and fulfilment, but it is also economically viable. The creation, management and distribution of art employs many.

The connection between leadership and art has been made many times over, perhaps because certain properties of the arts do carry over to leadership. Let us look and learn about this very important sphere of leadership, but my point is more ambitious: leadership is an actual art, not metaphorically an art.

One man stands out as a leader in the sphere of visual arts and I share his story here to motivate and inspire us.

Tyler Perry

Tyler Perry excels at many things: he's a world-renowned producer, director, actor, screenwriter, author, songwriter, entrepreneur, employer, and philanthropist. But do you know who Tyler Perry is at his core, and what makes him a Leader Worth Following? As we began to learn more about the man behind the image, we discovered there was so much to share about his past, present and vision for the future. So, I chose three of the values most often used to describe Tyler, that exemplify the characteristics of a true leader, regardless of his title, industry or role:

Discipline

The odds for success were not in Tyler's favour. Even his teachers tried to dissuade his dreams, telling him he'd never make it. They told him he was "too dumb, too black, too poor." So, Tyler looked inward; he has said that he heard a still, small voice that told him he could do it. He didn't allow his critics to discourage him. Instead, he found a passion and drive to prove them wrong. Tyler overcame each obstacle he faced. Sometimes it took years, but he broke it down into daily discipline, work ethic and pure grit.

Authenticity

Tyler doesn't hide from the pain of his youth. Instead, he uses it as a source of inspiration and connection to others. He taps into the hurts of his upbringing as a source of authentic storytelling that inspires a loyal fan following. Tyler's creative spark was driven by his need to keep those he loved safe, and it grew into a mighty flame that did indeed help lift his mother out of poverty and abuse. It didn't stop there; Tyler's willingness to be open and his dedication to creating new work has become a point of inspiration and economic opportunity for many.

Beyond You

Due in part to his upbringing, Tyler has found a variety of ways to give back to his community and the world. He regularly contributes to and works with Hosea Feed the Hungry, Charity: Water, Global Medical

Relief Fund, and Feeding America, among other organizations. His foundation – The Tyler Perry Foundation, focuses on turning "tragedy into triumph," particularly in the areas of education, women's rights, clean water, and globally sustainable economic development. His "beyond you" leadership style is also evident on his movie sets.
Infused With Inspiration: A Leader in the making

As I researched and curated the insightful, inspiring leaders from a variety of industries, roles, backgrounds, and more, I could not help but be inspired by so many of them. Yes, I wanted these leaders that inspired me to move you and motivate you; but more than that, it is my desire for you to be armed with clear, tactical steps and solutions that you can apply to your own leadership growth.

I see Tyler Perry as the person to do just that. More than an entertainer, we see a leader in business, in his community, in his faith, and in his purpose to create an inclusive culture.

With so many ventures, Tyler is a testimony to singularity of purpose. He knows how to align his gifts and creative energy with a dedicated focus. That focus has made him one of the most prolific writers of the last 20 years – and he doesn't plan on slowing down any time soon. In fact, he has said that he is in continual growth mode.

Observing Tyler's vast media empire and entrepreneurial successes, you might assume that he was an overnight success. Far from it. Tyler did not travel an easy road. In 1992, after scrimping and saving his earnings from a variety of jobs, Tyler made the audacious move of producing his own stage production called I Know I've Been Changed, renting out the popular 14th Street Playhouse in Atlanta, known for its support of emerging artists. The way Tyler saw it was if 1,200 people came to his show over the weekend, he could recoup his investment. Instead, only 30 people attended the production, all of them friends and family.

Still, he did not quit. His faith did not falter. Yes, he had his moments of disillusion, disappointment and discontentment. But at every turn, Tyler's failures only strengthened his resolve and purpose. And six years later, that same production played to a sold-out audience at Atlanta's historic Fox Theatre.

He went on to introduce the world to the now-beloved character of Madea, first on the stage in his 1999 production, I Can Do Bad All By Myself; and then on the big screen in his 2005 film, Diary of a Mad Black Woman. The combination of perseverance and purpose helped make Tyler's dreams a reality.

Lupita Nyong'o

Lupita is one actress who continues to push boundaries for leadership. Nyong'o's first major TV break was her role in Shuga, a series that pushed the limits of global dialogue about sex and dating in Africa and advocated for HIV awareness. Her character was edgy, beautiful and a risk-taker, teaching audiences lessons about promiscuity, ambition and sexual safety. The show aired in 40 African countries as well as in the U.S., and was a hit, garnering a 2010 World Media Festival honour in Hamburg, Germany.

She did not rest on her laurels after winning an Oscar but has used her popularity to mentor young girls. Leadership is about influence and this young actress has influenced young girls to read, to think and discuss issues that are important to them and in my thinking that is what leadership is all about. Beyond talking about Black is Beautiful she has embraced her dark skin leading young girls and women to celebrate who they are without wanting to change and conform to what society says they should be. In my opinion, Lupita is a leader on so many fronts.

I could write a whole book on leaders in the visual arts who have influenced me, and I believe you could do the same. When we learn to live in a way that is a testament to how they have influenced us, then we honour them as we should.

Chapter 12

The Influence of Literature on Leadership

Words are powerful. They inspire us, launch us into action, and they drive us to create the changes we want to see in the world.

Most of what I learned about leadership in my early years I learned from literature, and more particularly from books by African Authors.

Chinua Achebe
His classic, Things Fall Apart, is a story of leadership, intuition, and social transformation. It is one of the great works of modern literature. Chinua Achebe himself passed away, but his influence on novels, on writing, and also on thinking about the colonial past of Nigeria, of Africa – in fact, about colonialism in general, about the experience of being taken over, about the experience of culture and the ways of doing things, falling apart and needing change, and what leadership has to do with that. This great story and set of themes has been hugely influential in both literature and academic theory.

In Achebe's Things Fall Apart, the tragic protagonist Okonkwo responds to his surroundings by becoming a fierce, autocratic and reactionary leader. So embedded and unconscious is his behaviour, that he is unable to prevent himself from shooting at his wife, murdering his young protégé and decapitating a colonial messenger. Ironically, the characteristics of the 'great man' he seeks to be – strong, unwavering and ruthless – are also those that result in his inevitable downfall. What Okonkwo lacks is the power of introspection, adaptability and self-awareness. Characteristics he would no doubt dismiss as 'womanly'.

Recent studies indicate that women outperform men in leadership positions perhaps because they have higher emotional intelligence. Despite these studies, we remain more comfortable with 'powerful' and autocratic leaders.

Although we may empathise, Okonkwo is not alone in embodying a leadership style that's past its sell-by date. We must demand more from our leaders in today's increasingly complex and globalised environment. Without a strong awareness of self, adaptability and introspection, we are unwittingly following our evolutionary past – in essence, the traditions of our forefathers. Okonkwo serves as a grave warning of where that might just lead.

Ngugi wa Thiong'o and Ken Saro Wiwa

Known as literary giants each in their own right, Ngugi Wa Thiong'o and Ken Saro Wiwa led in the protection of indigenous communities' land rights in Kenya and Nigeria, respectively. They both used their literary platforms to highlight the wrongs perpetrated by capitalists and greedy politicians alongside the Kamiriithu and Ogoni communities in 1976 – 1982 and 1990 - 1995, respectively.

In the case of Kenya, the Kamiriithu community did not attain their land rights and other freedoms following the Ngugi-led activism.

Instead, the Kenyan government turned to further repression of individual and collective rights. In Nigeria, Saro-Wiwa was hanged after a trial marred with irregularities.

However, oil exploitation activities on land belonging to the Ogoni ceased. There has been progress in holding Shell legally accountable for environmental degradation and a study on the extent of damage done to the ecology has been undertaken. Both writers, despite different outcomes to their activism, played leadership roles in their communities' struggle for land rights. Their creative writing abilities and achievements played a role in their emergence as leaders and strategies for leadership.

Ngugi's repertoire of books makes him one of the most powerful leaders in African literature, his influence on students of literature and political science is second to none. The prizewinning Weep Not, Child is the story of a Kikuyu family drawn into the struggle for Kenyan independence during the state of emergency and the Mau Mau rebellion. A Grain of Wheat (1967), generally held to be artistically more mature, focuses on the many social, moral, and racial issues of the struggle for independence and its aftermath.

A third novel, The River Between (1965), which was actually written before the others, tells of lovers kept apart by the conflict between Christianity and traditional ways and beliefs and suggests that efforts to reunite a culturally divided community by means of Western education are doomed to failure. Petals of Blood (1977) deals with social and economic problems in East Africa after independence, particularly the continued exploitation of peasants and workers by foreign business interests and a greedy indigenous bourgeoisie.

There is no question that literary greats including Shakespeare, Albert Camus, Alex La Guma, have influenced the world, their pen more powerful than the gun or any podium to change the course of history.

Alex La Guma remains one of my favourite authors. He was a black novelist from South Africa in the 1960s whose characteristically brief works, A Walk in the Night (1962), The Stone-Country (1965), and In the Fog of the Season's End (1972) gained power through his superb eye for detail, allowing the humour, pathos, or horror of a situation to speak for itself.

La Guma was reared in a family active in the black liberation movement. In 1960 he joined the staff of the progressive newspaper New Age. During the next few years, he was detained and imprisoned several times for his antiapartheid activities. The South African government banned his writing and speaking, and in 1966 he and his family moved to London, where he lived in exile until 1979. In his later years, he served as the representative of the African National Congress, ANC in Cuba.

His first novel, A Walk in the Night, presents the struggle against oppression by a group of characters in Cape Town's toughest district and, in particular, the moral dissolution of a young man who is unjustly fired from his job. Its general theme of protest is reiterated in And a Threefold Cord (1964), which depicts the degrading effect of apartheid upon a ghetto family, and in The Stone-Country, which grew out of La Guma's experiences in prison. His short stories appeared in many anthologies and magazines. The novel Time of the Butcherbird appeared in 1979. La Guma's high reputation is based on his vivid style, his colourful dialogue, and his ability to present sympathetically and realistically people living under sordid and oppressive circumstances.

Other authors have left an indelible mark on my mind regarding leadership, among them, Brené Brown.

In The Gifts of Imperfection, Brown is candid and qualitative on how striving for perfection sets us up for unhappiness. She shows that the number one reason people are happy is because they feel worthy and belong. Conversely, the number one reason people are not happy is because they feel unworthy and alone. This is a powerful message for leaders. Think of where our employee engagement scores would be if people felt they were part of a purposeful team where they truly belonged and were valued.

48 Laws of Power by Robert Greene – At first this book may make you bristle. All the more reason you should read it. This is certainly not a book on servant leadership for which I am a strong advocate. On the contrary, you need to know the hard realities of the work world and how others approach leadership to define how you will be authentic in the midst of any culture. I can't underscore enough the value of Rule #1: 'Never Outshine the Master. Always make those above you feel comfortably superior.' This sounds obsequious. Still, your boss needs to trust you and know you have his or her back. He or she is the single most influencer to help you advance. Aligned together, you can accomplish far more than if you are at odds.

Another of my favourite books that has had a great impact on how I view leadership is The Way of the Seal by Mark Divine. This ex-Navy seal shows us the importance of self-awareness in leadership. Your 'sentinel' is your witness to your thoughts. Divine suggests that you use your sentinel to have front site focus as if a sharpshooter. You must know what is unique about you – your 'unique offer' as a leader. Then simplify internal and external environments. Use visualization exercises to practice what it is like to live in the space of excellence. Repeatedly envision the specific details of success.

I am persuaded that to be a good leader, one must love reading, be an avid reader of a wide array of subjects. In fact, come to think of it, these authors are able to write well on leadership because they, themselves, are leaders in their particular spheres of influence.

Chapter 13

Teachers are Leaders

The central pillar of leadership is the ability to teach.

The English philosopher John Locke was staunch in his belief that knowledge should be passed on, and that development of character was the most important thing for people to learn.

The Greek philosopher Aristotle was the teacher of Alexander the Great and wrote on a number of subjects including metaphysics, poetry, and zoology.

Confucius, the great Chinese thinker, was a strong advocate for personal and governmental morality, whose teachings greatly influenced Chinese, Korean, Japanese and Vietnamese culture.

These historical icons are still referenced by many throughout the world, and their influence points strongly to what may be the central pillar of leadership: the ability to teach.

Business magnate Warren Buffett has offered his pearls of wisdom to Microsoft owner, Bill Gates through the years; Steve Jobs was a guiding light for Facebook's Mark Zuckerberg; and iconic songwriter Bob

Dylan developed his unique style thanks to the support of music legend, Woody Guthrie.

Throughout the ages, even the greatest of leaders have benefited from the guidance of teachers, and many became prominent teachers in their own right, as seen in the example of Aristotle, who was taught by Plato, who was in turn taught by Socrates.
Teacher leadership is both a right and responsibility of all teaching professionals. Throughout their often-diverse careers, most teachers maintain many leadership roles. They may help other teachers improve their ability to instruct students, or they may lead teams to better meet the needs of the students, school and community. Above all, they are great influencers of future leaders.

Teacher leaders assume a wide range of roles to support school and student success. Whether these roles are assigned formally or shared informally, they build the entire school's capacity to improve. Because teachers can lead in a variety of ways, many teachers do serve as leaders among their peers.

Teachers exhibit leadership in multiple, sometimes overlapping, ways. Some leadership roles are formal with designated responsibilities. Other more informal roles emerge as teachers interact with their peers. The variety of roles ensures that teachers can find ways to lead that fit their talents and interests. Regardless of the roles they assume, teacher leaders shape the culture of their schools, improve student learning, and influence practise among their peers.

Skilled teachers have the power to make a real difference in the lives of students. But educators who exemplify leadership skills within the field are able to make an even greater impact. Teachers who learn to translate their successful classroom practices into a shared vision that can help drive the school, the district or even the industry forward can benefit students far beyond their classrooms.

Teachers have an extraordinary opportunity to exercise leadership because they are the most powerful influence, next to students, on other teachers' practice. Where principals can shape teachers' beliefs, attitudes, and behaviours, other teachers do shape them.

Principals need teacher leaders of all kinds. Great schools grow when educators understand that the power of their leadership is in the strength of their relationships. While school administrators play an important and vital role in improving relationships and outcomes for students, teachers are uniquely positioned to contribute and have developed special assets that enhance the school leadership mix.

Teacher leaders have the expertise and are compelled to share with others. Teachers everywhere should be committed to the growth of their students, certainly, and equally committed to the growth of each other. It is no longer acceptable for teachers to learn something and become expert at it (for example project-based learning, readers' workshop, hand on geometry, technology use, etc.) and be limited to the four walls of the classroom. When teachers and teaching remain private the school's instructional capacity remains static or diminishes. Neither scenario is acceptable.

I am very conscious that understandings of leadership work undertaken by teachers typically reinforce those with formal positional roles at the expense of other forms of leadership which I believe are equally important for the improvement of student learning and achievement in schools. I use the term informal or teacher leadership to acknowledge the leadership work undertaken by teachers without titles and incentives of time and remuneration. In so doing, I favour a collective rather than individual interpretation of leadership, where it is the work which matters rather than a person holding power, status and superiority over others.

My view is that many teachers engage in leadership work which either they or others may not necessarily recognise as leadership. Informal leadership by teachers is harder to distinguish because of its close connection to teachers acting professionally and continuing to deepen their understandings of what it takes to help students to learn. This type of leadership emerges when teachers see interactions with colleagues as opportunities to make sense of practice accepting a mutual exchange of insights, with each moving between leading and learning according to their expertise. In this way, learning to improve teaching is the impetus for leadership.

However, how we acknowledge this leadership and learning connection in terms of language remains a difficulty because who counts as this type of leader is always a tension when highlighting the collective rather than individual space in which teachers lead. I now favour teachers as leaders because I have realised that without the word 'teachers' in the terminology, there is no recognition of the greater number of the profession who are engaging in leadership work.

Research has clearly told us the leadership qualities and behaviours that are most effective. We know very well what distinguishes good leaders from mediocre and bad leaders. But a question that often arises is whether or not teachers (from elementary school through college) are actually "leaders." I'm going to stop short of saying "yes," because we tend to use the term "leader" too broadly already. What I can say definitively, however, is that the very best teachers behave very much like the very best leaders. In other words, successful teachers are very much like successful leaders - they both engage in transformational behaviours.

Transformational leadership is the most popular theory today. It consists of four key components. Let's look at how outstanding teachers - we will call them "transformational teachers" - display these four key elements.

Idealized Influence: Successful leaders are positive role models for followers. Followers of transformational leaders admire their leaders and try to emulate their positive and authentic behaviour. So too, transformational teachers are much admired by their students. A common reason given for pursuing a teaching career is being impressed by a transformational teacher and desiring to follow in his or her footsteps.

Inspirational Motivation: Transformational teachers, like transformational leaders, are positive and inspirational. They are enthusiastic about what they are doing, and that enthusiasm infects their students. Students are motivated to work hard. My daughter's 4th-grade teacher personified this element of transformational teaching/leading. He was lively, sang to the kids, and on school outings, he looked like he was having the most fun of all.

Individualized Consideration: This element is one of the strongest drivers of transformational leadership, and the same is true for transformational teaching. It involves the leader, or teacher, being attuned to the individual needs of each follower/student. It is a genuine concern for what each person needs to develop fully. Individually considerate teachers coach and mentor each student, providing that individual attention that helps the student succeed.

Intellectual Stimulation. Perhaps this element is even more important for teachers than for leaders; it involves challenging students/followers to engage their minds and to think creatively. The very best teachers get students to think about things in new ways and challenge them to greater intellectual achievements. They encourage creative and novel thinking, rather than discouraging it.

So, the theory of transformational leadership seems to apply very well to teachers. We know for sure that outstanding teachers, whether or not they are actually 'leaders' in the regular use of the word, play a key role in the development of future leaders. There is not a leader in the world that did not have a great teacher somewhere along their path to leadership.

Many teachers sow the seeds of greatness into their students who then grow to become great leaders. Leadership inspires, encourages, motivates, and sets an overall vision.

But leaders don't last forever, and those who come after them – if legacies are to mean anything – have to know how to carry on that legacy by becoming leaders themselves.

This is why the best leaders are often great teachers because they are aware of the need to pass on their knowledge in a way that not only motivates their followers, but also empowers them to do whatever needs to be done in order for progress to flourish.

Alexander the Great once said of Aristotle:

I am indebted to my father for living, but to my teacher for living well.

Chapter 14

Leaders in Sports

If you want to be a better leader, you need to make that decision now…
Decide now and begin practicing how to lead your team well.
PGC

Leadership development in sport focuses on developing four central components: high skill, strong work ethic, enriched cognitive sport knowledge, and good rapport with people.

Sport is the second most lucrative industry in North America, and it has gotten there through audacious leadership by the athletes themselves, coaches and franchise owners. Whether it is from a coach, manager, or teammate, the demand for effective leadership to increase performance is an ever-present phenomenon in the domain of sport.

Let us look at some of the top leaders in the various sport codes whether they are individual sports like golf or team sports like basketball or rugby. Sports provides intense, no-nonsense training for players and coaches, teaching players of all positions to play smart on the court, and be leaders in practices, games and in everyday life.

Training to be a Leader

Point Guard College is a basketball education camp that fosters leadership on and off the court and attracts players from across the country.

"Not everyone can be the star of the team, but everyone can star in their role." ~ Doc Rivers

One of the things I love about basketball is that it has showcased some incredible leaders on and off the court. They include:

Kobe Bryant

Famous for his double-digit scores including 60 points in his final game, five NBA Championship rings, 18-time All-Star, 15-time member of the All-NBA Team, 12-time member of the All-Defensive Team, 2008 NBA Most Valuable Player (MVP), two-time NBA Finals MVP winner, Kobe retired and went on to lead in the world of business and entertainment until his untimely death in January 2020.

Though blessed with exceptional talent, Kobe's leadership abilities were honed through tireless commitment to grow as an athlete, person, and leader. His loss transcends the realm of sports, and his leadership agility can be a beacon to all aspiring leaders regardless of field.

Tiger Woods

Announced as a finalist for the 2021 induction into the World Golf Hall of Fame, Tiger's emergence onto the PGA TOUR was swift and monumental. When he won the Masters in 1998, he violently shook the last embers of prejudice from the game of golf. His ability to do so prove without a doubt that one's skin colour has little to do with one's proficiency in the game of golf. Augusta National was transformed from a place of only black caddies and white players into the historical stage of unbiased universal acceptance. Tiger Woods transcended the game of golf to impact the thoughts, words, and behaviour of people outside the game. And that is what leadership is all about as we have seen consistently throughout this book.

Serena Williams

Serena Williams is a great leader in her field. Serena not only supports her country but helps lives around the world. Serena helps to raise money for the fundraisers Build African Schools, UNICEF and World Education that really helped kids. Serena became a leader for always encouraging other players to never give up.

As a leader, Serena Williams has all kinds of different qualities. The one habit of the mind that I think Serena Williams has is Persistence. I think she has persistence because she always has a back-up plan, stays strong, never gives up and always tries her best.
Serena Williams is a very important leader. Ms Williams stands up against different things, like sexism and racism. She also shows that pregnancy shouldn't stop you from working in your career.

Throughout Serena Williams' career, she had to deal with a lot of hatred against her, especially as a woman. In 2018, she lost a tournament. During a game, she was getting angry because the umpire kept wrongfully accusing her of "violations" that she did not commit. She felt deeply offended by the umpire saying she was "cheating" and being coached on the side. Later, after she lost the game, she broke her bracket and the umpire took a point from Williams, even though the game was over. On the other hand, Nick Kyrigosin, a male tennis player, showed similar behaviour in a 2019 game and didn't face any penalties.

In response to backlash about her behaviour, Serena stated, *"Why can't I express my frustrations like everyone else? If I were a man, would I be in this situation? What makes me so different? Is it because I'm a woman? I stop myself to avoid getting worked up. I tell myself, 'You've been through so much, you've endured so much, time will allow me to heal, and soon this will be just another memory that made me the woman, mother, and athlete I am now."* This shows Serena is a leader because she doesn't let anyone, especially men, tell her she's not great because she knows who she is and what she is capable of.

Finally, Serena is an inspiration to women. In 2016 Serena Williams played in the Australian Open while pregnant. She left an impact on young women because she showed them that even if they are pregnant, they can still do things. She supported that by winning a whole tournament while she was pregnant.

Serena Williams is a very important leader. She stands up for what she knows is right and believes in. Serena has been through it all and has been able to learn from her experiences. She's gotten through racism, sexism, and has been able to stay on top of her game.

Whether in sports or in life, teams and communities desire and need leadership. In difficult times players are left searching out the leaders in their team, but not everyone can pick up to the baton and lead a team. It takes a special range of characteristics to excel as a sports leader. If you want to be a leader for your team, community or country, here are some important things to keep in mind and pursue:

Determine what your role is

Depending on your role in the team your scope for leadership can change, and the series of pointers given below will be realised in slightly different ways.

Coaches can use the training ground and pre-and-post match team talks to display their leadership, but once the players are out on the field, it's generally down the captain. Captains are responsible for taking what their coach does off the field and implementing it on match day.

Coaches and captains are obviously the first place to look for leadership, but they aren't the only ones who can take the bull by the horns on-or-off the field. Leadership can come from any team member on the pitch. Keep in mind what we learned at the very beginning of the book in chapter two: Leadership is not positional.

Develop the right skills, and you could be the one delivering a killer injection of leadership to lift your team from potential defeat to dramatic victory. Again, bear in mind your individual role within the team and how you might use the pointers given here to display true leadership.

Set an example

As a leader and authority figure, your fellow team members are likely to follow you down any behavioural path you choose. For the good of the team then, you need to be heading down the right pathway. If you're seen with your head down, ranting and raving at players or officials, or generally negatively conducting yourself, then your players will see no reason why they can't behave in exactly the same manner. The best leaders are the hardest workers on the pitch or gym and the most respectful of their sport.

The same goes for training days and off the field commitments. Turning up late or having a less than enthusiastic attitude to training is just giving the rest of your team a reason to take their eye of the ball. Set a good example, and your team will feed off your enthusiasm and positivity to give you the best chance of achieving your goals.

Awareness

As the leader of a team, awareness is key. There's no absolute method to leadership, and your approach to certain scenarios should be heavily influenced by external factors. Awareness comes through time spent building relationships with your teammates, peers and players. Learn how they react to certain styles and tones. If you are on the end of a serious defeat, do they react better to a few harshly spoken words, or do they need an arm around their shoulder to help them lick their wounds?

It works on an individual basis too. Certain players react differently to different kinds of leadership. A passionate, rousing team talk may be enough to get most players up before a big game, but others may just need a few softer motivational cues in their ear to get them in the zone or back on track.

In the heat of the moment, it is easy to lose sight of your awareness of the situation, leading to you taking the wrong tone with teammates. Develop it by drawing on what you know about your team, individual players, the match or training scenario and previous experiences in similar situations.

Passion

Sport is intrinsically passionate. You feel the same set of emotions out on the pitch every weekend: euphoria from victory and disappointment in defeat. As a leader, you have to embody the positive side of those emotions (commitment, dedication and passion) to drive your team towards their goals. It's not just passion towards victory you need to display as a leader.

Caring for your teammates and your sport from a wider perspective are both ways you can show passion. It's not all about fist-pumping and over-exuberant celebrations; passion can be about showing compassion for your teammates or respecting the opposition.

Enthusiasm

A quality similar to passion, enthusiasm is an important characteristic for a leader and one that can be displayed in a number of ways.

On the pitch, enthusiasm is being the first to every ball, offering encouragement to your fellow players, or geeing up your team when they are looking down and out. But encouragement also stretches to your day-to-day behaviour as a sports leader and can often be more valuable in the long run.

Show enthusiasm for your game as an individual and towards the sport you love and expect others to follow. Be the most enthusiastic in training; be enthused to new ideas; be supportive of team bonding activities; strive to be the best out on the pitch or gym every weekend.

Enthusiasm is infectious. Injecting some into everything you do when representing your team can lead to an increase in dedication and commitment from everyone involved in your team.

Ability

Leaders, and in this case particularly coaches, live and die by their decision-making. As the creator and implementor of a strategy off the field, or key figure in decision making on it, you need to have the knowledge and ability to stand by the strength of your convictions.

Leaders are often elevated into their position because of their ability (particularly team captains). Without that ability, your authority can become undermined. Strive to improve your skills, and not only will it leave you in a better position to lead, but it'll also set an example to others to improve their game.

Communicate

Communication is a vital area in team sport. And if any member of the team needs to nail it down, it's the leaders of the team. At the very core of great leadership is inspiring others towards a series of goals. To get those goals across to team members, you need to be able to communicate them effectively. Make it clear to your players what you want to achieve and how you intend them to contribute to achieving it. Clear, concise communication can really boost your success rate as a leader.

Again, awareness is an important factor that ties in with communication. You know the players that you lead better than anyone, so learn to take the right communicative approach for each of them.

Motivational skills

Honing your motivational skills should be a top priority as you look to become a better leader. Not only can it squeeze out those little margins between winning and losing, but it challenges players to be better every day.

Good leadership is about infusing that challenge in the minds of your players. Motivate them to be better every day, and watch your team grow as a result.

Will to win

One final common theme runs through the finest sports leaders: an insatiable will to win. Good leaders are the ones that win every 50/50, bring their absolute best when the team needs it, pushes their teammates on and never gives an inch to the opposition.

Bringing energy to everything they do as they hunt out victory, leaders are winners as they put the required time and effort into what needs to be done to win. As long as these ruthless character traits don't' spill over into aggression or the use of unethical methods of victory, a complete and utter will to win should be high on the list of must-haves for sports leadership.

Visionary

They say that the best leaders lead from behind their men. Especially relevant to leadership in coaching, your job is plan out that vision in your own head before imprinting it into the minds of your team.

Many of the characteristics required to be a successful sports leader interlock with one another. Whenever you call upon them, do so as another step on the ladder to your over-arching vision. At the start of a leadership journey, use it as a constant source of motivation.

Your vision requires the ability to know how to get there, communication to let others know how they will contribute to success, and motivation and enthusiasm to share your vision and win the support of others.
Without knowing where your end game is, your capacity to lead is seriously diminished. Outline a series of goals for you and your team and use everything else in your leadership armoury to steer them towards it.

Leaders might be made in sports, but they continue to lead long after the final whistle is blown.

Chapter 15

Concluding Thoughts on Leadership

Leadership is a complex and challenging role. It is defined as the ability to empower followers through guidance, example, encouragement and compassion.

Throughout this book, I offer insights and perspectives on what I believe are some of the most important things one needs to do, consistently, and to keep in mind to be a great leader.

I have also paid tribute to leaders that I admire, leaders that have influenced me and leaders that inspire me. I have not delved into poor and bad leadership because I know and understand that "as a man thinketh, so is he…" a Biblical principle I adhere to strictly.

Leadership is not a new idea. Civilizations throughout all history recognized leaders and celebrated good leaders in a variety of forms. Generals like Julius Caesar, artists like Wagner and Shakespeare, philosophers like Socrates and social justice advocates like Malcolm X and Martin Luther King Jr., all have been lauded for possessing the qualities and characteristics of leadership. I have shed light on aspects of leadership development, transformational leadership and comparatively, servant leadership.

Our society depends on the abilities of our leaders and how well they do their jobs. A leader is someone that many people look to for direction, guidance, and inspiration, so it is important for our leaders to have the aptitude to make difficult decisions and to know and do what is right for the people. A higher authority is crucial for supervising and regulating others as well as being an example of hard work and dedication. An effective leader has character, competence, compassion, and courage.

Character is possibly the most important characteristic of a leader. A person's true character is who they are when they are put in a difficult situation. It is the decisions and the morality of a leader that gives them the respectable character that others look to follow. It is essential for a leader to have character because a leader needs the ability to see what others cannot, the sacrifices that must be made, even if the sacrifice is their own.

The second characteristic is competence. Having Competence means that one knows what must be done. It is possessing the skills to do one's task properly. This quality is vital for a leader because they are the people that command others. If they themselves do not know what their job is, it will be difficult to properly instruct others.

Thirdly, Compassion is important for a leader to have because when the people see that the leader cares for them, they will be more trusting of the decisions that he makes. Also, recognizing and taking the time to acknowledge them will make the people want to do their job properly and to the best of their ability. They will know that the leader is concerned with each person's weaknesses and will take them into account when making decisions. True compassion from a leader will inevitably lead to trust from their followers.

The fourth aspect of an effective leader is courage. Courage is described as having the strength both mentally and physically to do something that most people cannot or will not do. It is imperative for a leader to have courage because as a leader, they have to make decisions that impact people's lives. It takes true courage to not only make the decision but also to stand by it.

So, in conclusion, an effective leader must have character, competence, compassion, and courage. These characteristics are the components of one's personality that gives them the capability to successfully lead a group of people in the right direction. Character allows you to make the right choices. Competence is the ability to know your job and what needs to be done. Compassion is a fairness and respect for other leaders and your followers. And lastly, courage is both mental and physical strength to do what is right even though it may be the hardest. These characteristics are what makes a leader worth following and worthy of recognition as a leader.

Other books by the Author

1.The Mind Set - You Are What YOU Think
ISBN - 13978-0-620- 75973-1

2. The Success Codes: The Last Human Hope (2017)
ISBN - 13978-0-620-77926-5

3. Determinants of Success ~ Na'anlep's Persuasive Thinking
ISBN - 978-1-990966-17-0

Upcoming book

Paradigm Shift (Mental Revolution)

Introduction

This is a pattern or mannequin model of intellectual revolution and transformation which must serve as the bedrock for every significant development and productiveness via every country focused on a stable future at all spheres of its country wide of life.

It could be for the cause of changing lives, transforming nations and intellectual ability if a human resource of countries at a number of levels and phases of growth and development.

Nothing can stop a country or a man with the right intellectual mindset from accomplishing a desire, targets, goals and objectives. Nothing on earth can help a country or a man with the wrong intellectual mindset or disposition to achieve greatness.

Every generation, every country or continent needs an innovative, revolutionary and transformational shift in mental potential to impact the desired heights. To that end, there is an urgent need for mental revolution and transformation; a radical shift in the way we see the world around us and do things. This will equip us to meaningfully impact people's lives and therefore the world in order to create a symbolic and symbiotic value chain for upcoming generations.

The human thought remains the most important vehicle to drive significant growth and development. The mind-set is the seat of wisdom, ideas and factory of greatness. Every change must commence from within and reflect on the outside. The human mind, I have found, is limitless in its capacity.

Raymond Delmut Na'anlep

The author is also available for speaking engagements:
galaxymediahouse@gmail.com
Cell: +234 803 653 2529